Ton

# Brain Tumours, John Bonham and Fat Pigeons

Copyright ©2024, Tom Shaw
Tom Shaw asserts the moral right to be identified as the author of this book.

ISBN: 9798883660947

All rights reserved. No part of this publication may be reproduced, stored in a retrieval system, or transmitted in any form or by any means, electronic, mechanical, photocopying, recording or otherwise, without the prior permission of the author.

This book is sold subject to the condition that it shall not, by way of trade or otherwise, be lent, re-sold, hired out or otherwise circulated without the author's prior consent in any form of binding or cover other than that in which it is published and without a similar condition including this condition being imposed on the subsequent purchaser.

# Brain Tumours, John Bonham and Fat Pigeons

# *Introduction*

It's here!

I'm pleased to say the book that nobody demanded, about somebody you don't know has arrived. So those of you that didn't know you wanted it can stop not wanting it...

On November 26th, 2007, I had a 'relatively straightforward' brain tumour removed. Not much of a story, except that it turned out to be inoperable. And then the surgeon operated anyway[1].

---

[1] As it was this or dying, I figure I came out ahead.

Oh, and you need to know that I'm an idiot. I always forget to mention that. I thought I should tell you this because you might be reading this and think 'hmmm, idiot, or not idiot?' And I feel as though, as I'm in a wheelchair, you'll feel obliged to think 'not an idiot'. So, to save you discomfort, let me say it for you.

The fact is my current condition is largely self-inflicted because of my desire to handle everything on my own and not ask for help. The problem with this is that by not talking to people, I'm relying on my own advice and, as we've established, I'm an idiot. I ignored all the signs and alarm bells for too long. My reward was a year in hospital, years of speech therapy, years of physiotherapy and this book.

Does that make me a hero? It's saying things like this that make me an idiot, isn't it?

I'd seen numerous doctors, visited Accident & Emergency, been advised to see a dentist. and eventually collapsed before I could get an MRI. Then a neurosurgeon told me that the tumour was "away from all the major clockwork". I'd need about twelve weeks of physio and then I would be back to how I was before.

This isn't how it turned out. The inaccuracy of the prognosis wasn't the neurosurgeon's fault, or the fault of the two other neurosurgeons who saw my case later.

I won't go into too much detail here though as this is meant as an intro. I did put it all down in a blog, but few people read it. I expected millions of hits; visitors would tell their friends and every single person they told would log on and read and also tell all of their friends. I thought I would get thousands of new readers each week.

I didn't.

It takes me a long time to type nowadays, so this continuous flow of posts required me to write a post and then immediately start writing the next post so that there wasn't much waiting in between posts. I didn't want to leave the millions of people waiting too long for the next part of my magnum opus. So in order to fulfil my self-inflicted deadline I'd leave out important details; there'd be spelling and grammar mistakes; I'd write sentences that directly contradicted something I'd previously said. I felt under immense pressure to give my millions of adoring fans what they wanted.

If at first you don't succeed…

The blog did fill a function though. It gave me the order of things that happened in what's turned out to be, literally, a series of life-changing journeys.

This book is my attempt at putting those ramblings into something more readable. There are no guarantees it'll turn out that way, but let's find out together.

…but don't forget: I'm an idiot.

## Chapter 1
## *Hurty Heads, Dodgy Doctors and Losing Consciousness*

I had been going to bed with a fan facing me and blasting cold air into my face as I was too hot to get to sleep. I'd been doing this a lot lately, this had started around the beginning of summer (maybe even as far back as spring), I didn't put the fan on every night as I wasn't always too hot, but as time went on it became a necessary habit. It wasn't a cause for concern at first because it had been quite a warm summer, now it was approaching winter, in England, a country that isn't famed for its good weather. Should this have rung alarm bells? If you are constantly hot at night, your first thought isn't going to be 'I might have a tumour! Best see a doctor.' It's reasonable to try things like sleeping with a thinner duvet, or no duvet, or wearing less in bed. In isolation this wouldn't be a concern but everything I'm going to tell you obviously points to something serious.

With the benefit of hindsight I now realise that this was the early signs of the tumour. I don't think it had fully formed yet though, and If I had gone to a doctor at this point I imagine I would have been told "it's nothing" as had been the case on several occasions. If I had managed to get it diagnosed then and there the outcome could have been as the neurosurgeon predicted some months later.

When I woke up in the morning I would sit on the side of the bed and wait for the pain in my head to start. Sitting up after many hours of lying down would start my head throbbing as regular as clockwork. It wasn't coming from the front of my head the way a headache normally does and the moment it came I stopped what I was doing and waited for it to stop. It wasn't any more painful than a regular headache and I could have carried on regardless of the discomfort but the fact that it didn't feel like a regular headache meant I would stop and wait for it to subside, which it always did. I would then go for a shower and found that just stepping into the bath (the shower was in the bath) would set the throbbing off. Again it was as regular as clockwork. Throughout the day various things would trigger the pain in my head. I was getting good at predicting what would set it off and avoided doing it. No need to solve a problem when you can avoid it, a belief that's served me well in my forty-plus years on the planet (as you can't sense tone when reading text, that was said with a big dollop of sarcasm).

What has become clear while writing this is that I rush everything, always have. When I was younger I wanted everything now, something that didn't have a consequence at first as the story below illustrates…

## An Idiot Doing Idiotic Things

I had a year-old Renault Clio and I was barely affording the payments on it. I was looking on the Auto Express website one day, looking through all of the Renault Clio 172s and dreaming that I would one day be able to afford one. I couldn't believe it! One was available that I could afford!

It was dark blue/purple and I think all 172s at that time were black. This 172 was an import from the Republic of Ireland and had a custom paint job. I was in love and the sound of Mike Myers in Wayne's World saying "it will be mine, oh yes, it will be mine" echoed through my ears.

My current Renault Clio could just be handed back to the dealership with a small cancellation fee. I sorted out a loan with the bank and then arranged to withdraw the sum from my account. It was for a larger sum than the usual couple of hundred-pound ATM limit and so I had to go to the bank with ID and proof of address. I left the bank with the urgency of someone in dire need of the toilet, I was walking as fast as one can without running. Carrying a few thousand pounds in a jiffy bag suddenly makes you wary of everybody. That pensioner walking slowly holding onto a Zimmer frame could spring into life, nab the jiffy bag and sprint off like she's Usain Bolt.

Dad and I drove up to Leeds to see the car. I spoke to the seller for a very short time, gave the car the once-over - but didn't test drive it - and then asked him to give us a few minutes while we discussed the car. There wasn't any deliberation, it was just for show so that this guy didn't see me as an easy sale. Although the Renault Clio 172 tracksuit I was wearing probably hinted this was going to be easy. However, the idea of being a tough negotiator is different from actually being one. I suddenly lost my bottle and took the easy option and whipped out my jiffy bag full of cash and gave him exactly what the asking price was. It was the easiest money he'd ever made.

The only time I've attempted to negotiate is when I bought my house, I tried to low-ball them and start from a number lower than my limit, so I had room to negotiate. I'd seen this done on the telly so I knew this was a good tactic. Unfortunately what I hadn't seen on telly was the response I got.

"I'd like to buy the property, so I'll offer £xxx,xxx" I said confidently, starting the negotiation off at a figure I could increase as necessary.

"No, I'll accept £xxx,xxx which is the asking price" she replied, sensing my kryptonite is negotiating.

"I'll pay £xxx,xxx which is the asking price" I replied, as if I'd had a Jedi mind trick played on me.

On the drive back from Leeds in my newly acquired two litre pocket rocket I gave it the beans on the motorway and heard a rattle. It sounded like there were lots of bits of metal in the exhaust. That was a £500 visit to Kwik Fit. £500 I wouldn't have spent if I'd taken a breath and test driven it first.

Then I found out the insurance was going to cost more than I expected. I thought it was three years since my previous claim. It wasn't.

This dream car that I could *just* afford, that needed a new exhaust on the way home, was now going to cost me an extra £175.

I didn't have £175 so I was now going to be paying a loan off for a car I couldn't drive. My brother Adam, had recently come into some money and gave me the £175 meaning I was now paying £1600 to insure my hot hatch!

If it wasn't for these pesky teenagers having accidents as soon as they've passed and increasing the insurance premiums.

Oh that reminds me, I'll tell you later why I claimed when I was a pesky teenager…

## Back in Reality

I was a self-employed web developer at the time, so I could be quite flexible with my working hours. I found I was getting tired in the day, which again didn't ring alarm bells. It didn't even enter my mind that this was a problem. If I had a regular job I wouldn't have been able to just nap the problem away. But I didn't and I could. So I'd call "nap time" to my big black cat Molly and we'd have a nap for a couple of hours.

I tried drinking Red Bull to keep me awake, but I drank the energy drink directly before going to sleep, meaning I wouldn't even try to stay awake. It didn't dawn on me that the purpose of an energy drink is to give you energy and prevent you from going to sleep. However, I wouldn't feel tired after my nap and as far as I was concerned this was because of the combination of sleep and the energy drink. I was a genius!

I'd kept this tiredness – and my solution - to myself though. If I'd spoken to someone, they might have pointed out that what I was doing was counter-intuitive. It might even have led me to discussing my throbbing head and seeking help sooner.

My Dad and I went to my brother's (Daniel) house to watch Ricky Hatton (I think it was the Jose Luis Castillo fight) which would make it 23/06/2007. Daniel had Guitar Hero II and we spent the majority of the night playing it while we waited for the fight. A lot of silliness and hilarity ensued but I found that laughing uncontrollably was causing my head to throb, so I stopped joining in. The throbbing was still only as uncomfortable as a headache at this point, like when you have a hangover and your head is banging so you avoid loud noises. I didn't express major concern about this, probably saying something like "I'm going to stop, I've got a headache", down-playing the incident as something that would be remedied by swallowing a few pills.

This wouldn't have been concerning to Dad and Daniel. If I'd made a fuss about the overheating and tiredness, then said "I'm going to stop, I've got a headache", it would have led to questions; questions that I wouldn't be able to answer and as a result they'd have encouraged me to see a doctor.

I began to experience breathing problems. I was lying on my back on the sofa watching television when I suddenly had to take a deep breath. My regular breathing pattern didn't seem to be getting enough air in and the need for a deep breath was occurring several times. This did concern me; it wasn't occurring during the day while I was sitting up. I shared this with my girlfriend, Laura, and we thought that I should go to the doctor's.

When I saw the doctor, I didn't tell him about the other issues I'd been having. It's like those issues didn't exist now that I had a new issue to think about. This would have been the perfect opportunity to ask for some help. I didn't seize the opportunity though. If I'd told the Doctor the three other issues I had, this probably would have led to the tumour being discovered sooner. Obviously I didn't though.

The Doctor did a lung capacity test. From memory I think this involved blowing into a tube with a plastic ping-pong ball inside it. My memory is a bit hazy on this, I'm not entirely sure what the test was, but it didn't show anything out of the ordinary. To be safe though the Doctor booked me in for an assessment at the hospital and prescribed an inhaler. At the hospital I did another lung capacity test, although the likelihood of it showing any different results seemed pretty slim I thought. I then saw a neurosurgeon who sent me on my way without any concerns.

'Great!' I thought.

I didn't pursue the matter further because I hadn't connected the dots yet. I'd got the result I wanted and it didn't cause me any inconvenience. If I'd been as concerned as any other person would have been, I would have refused to be dismissed and demanded an MRI scan. Failing that I should have gone straight back to my Doctor and asked for something else.

With a clean bill of health, I started going to the gym to try and get in shape. I used to go to the gym a lot or not at all, depending on my commitment.

Recently I'd been in a not-at-all phase but a few years earlier I'd been in the shape of my life. I'd been going to the gym with a friend of mine who had similar goals of getting fit. What we started was about three years of going to the gym three or four times a week. We pushed each other to do more than the other. I'd constantly try to lift more and for longer. We were both quite evenly matched, but on some machines he would do a number of reps that I would struggle to match, but would push myself incredibly hard trying to. I didn't want to be outdone. Then one day I just stopped. Years of exercise and I just stopped.

I stopped my other activities like playing 5-a-side football and attending a weekly circuit-training class. Regular exercise can be quite boring and is a continuous necessity if you don't want everything you eat and drink to have a consequence on your appearance. If you're going to stop exercising you should at least adjust your diet accordingly, but you will always see and feel the effects. I continued to eat like I was regularly exercising, and I was drinking more as well and as a result I put on an alarming amount of weight, and quickly.

I decided I wanted to get back into shape and started going to the gym three times a week with the same friend. I'd start on the treadmill, but I found that running for the same amount of time as I used to was triggering my breathing difficulty, but strangely not my throbbing head. I'd use the inhaler afterwards but it had no effect. I was heavier though, so what could I expect, right? I might have been overweight now but surely the inhaler should have helped a little? Shouldn't that be concerning?

'Nah' I thought, 'on to the Smithy!'

The Smithy is similar to the bench-press you'll be familiar with, but it's away from the 'serious' weight trainers who usually congregate around the weight bench. It has a cord attached to the bar on either end. It doesn't give you all the benefits the free weight bench does as the Smithy supports the bar. But quite bad pains in my head would build for the duration I was using the Smithy, possibly because, when weight-training, the person tends to hold their breath and put a large amount of effort in to moving the weight.

The throbbing wouldn't completely subside while I was watching my mate taking his turn lifting the weights. I would then start my exercise already in pain, pain that built each time I pushed the bar up. It felt like my brain was going to explode. It was throbbing with such ferocity I could hear it in my ears and felt I might pass out.

This was one of the few occasions I was experiencing pain when lying on my back. I later learned that the pain of a brain tumour tends to present itself most when you're lying down, a symptom I didn't exhibit.

Fortunately when I was training on the Smithy, I always put 'stops' underneath the bar so the bar couldn't fall onto my neck if I let go of it. Maybe losing consciousness in this situation would have been a good thing. I couldn't have got hurt, I would have been in a room full of people, the staff would have had some medical knowledge and if I went to hospital the tumour may have been discovered before it became the problem it did.

I stopped going to the gym. Why solve the problem when you can just avoid it? Again, I didn't say anything to anyone - talking about my issues probably would have prompted the response "Go to the doctor!"

At the end of September 2007 I went to Turkey for a week with Laura. I took lots of Kool Strips and Anadin. Kool Strips are large pads that you stick against your forehead when you have a migraine. They contain blue gel and I think they're meant to be stored in a cooler place than in a bag in a hot hotel room. I'd come to the point where I was taking headache pills regularly and using the Kool Strips at least once every day, sometimes going up to the room for a little while to lie on the bed with a Kool Strip on my forehead. This didn't have any effect at all, but my head was bursting, and these were the only remedies I had available.

We'd taken a small Frisbee to chuck about in the pool. I was struggling with the pain, but generally we'd lie on a sun lounger and read a book, which I could manage. But it was extremely hot and the pool was cold, so we'd go in to cool off. It was a welcome shock to the system. We took the

Frisbee into the pool, but after about ten minutes I had to stop and get back on the sun lounger. Just looking up would result in ten seconds of intense pain. Unfortunately seeing where a Frisbee is, is an essential part of catching it. A young German girl of around seven years old joined us and we formed a triangle so that we could throw the Frisbee between us. I didn't want to make it obvious that looking up was painful as this might invite questions, so I'd glance up with one eye closed as you might when looking up at a bright sky. This seemed to work, I was feeling okay. The Frisbee was thrown to the girl, but it fell on the surface of the water some distance away from her. I dived forward, grabbed it and attempted to run away. She immediately jumped on my back and clasped around my neck to hold on. The throbbing in my head started again, but there was a language barrier so if I yelped in pain, I wouldn't be able to explain to her she hadn't done anything, I just gave her the Frisbee so she would get off, stood in the triangle for another few throws and then got out.

I was regularly in pain throughout the holiday and sometimes just doing regular things like having dinner or having a drink in a bar would trigger the pain. Up until now I'd been able to avoid situations that might trigger my problem, but soon the pain became almost constant. At last, I admitted to myself that something wasn't right and I needed to seek help when I got home.

## Doctor visit one

The first 'doctor' I saw did some coordination tests which consisted of closing my eyes and placing a finger on the tip of my nose. I'd put my hand in different positions, but was always able to find the tip of my nose. Next, I had to walk on an imaginary white line, putting one foot directly in front of the other, touching the tip of the toes on my standing foot with the heel of the other whilst looking straight ahead with my arms stretched out on either side. I didn't have any difficulties with this either.

He said there was nothing to worry about and put me on ten milligrams of Amitriptyline and told me to make another appointment if it wasn't helping. I tried it for a day and made another appointment as the medication had no effect. I was very concerned now and was acting as fast as I could.

## Doctor visit two

I saw a different 'doctor' the next time. There are many doctors at the surgery I go to. There is a doctor who I consider to be my doctor, and she is excellent. Unfortunately, many other people seem to be of the same opinion, so there was a wait to get to see her. As I'd finally realised there was a major problem, time was of the essence.

I explained the issues I was having to this second 'doctor'. I told him I'd seen another 'doctor' a few days ago. I explained that this 'doctor' had done some coordination tests, which I passed, and he sent me away with a small dose of Amitriptyline and the conclusion that it wasn't anything serious. This second 'doctor' said he would book me an appointment with a neurologist or an MRI scan, whichever came first.

He did neither and went on holiday.

## Doctor visit three

I made a third appointment this time seeing another 'doctor'. She upped my dose of Amitriptyline to 150mg and told me to try this dose for a few days and to come back and let her know if there's any change. I went back a few days later to let her know the increased dose of Amitriptyline hadn't helped.

## Doctor visit four

The 'doctor' who had increased my dose set about asking questions to find the cause, asking if I slept with one pillow or two, I said two so she suggested I sleep with one pillow from now on.

'Really?' I thought.

I didn't follow this advice, I carried on sleeping with two. I hope my dismissal of this excellent medical advice isn't to blame. Maybe people just need to change their sleeping habits to stop a brain tumour. (There I go with that sarcastic tone again.)

This was a load of nonsense I thought. I wish I'd kicked up a fuss:

"You've just upped my dose of Amitriptyline by 140mg and I'm telling you of several deeply concerning symptoms, do you really think this is all because of sleeping with two pillows?"

I wish I'd demanded an MRI scan.

She then asked me if I grind my teeth in my sleep and according to Laura I did. The 'doctor' thought this could be the reason for my headaches. Her suggestion was to go and see a dentist…

Unfortunately, this solution would likely cost me a great deal of money. I presume some moulds of my teeth would have been taken and a mouth guard would be fashioned, this would have taken weeks. I would have been in excruciating pain while I waited, several hundred pounds out of pocket and still requiring another visit to the 'doctor'.

I admit I ignored her expert advice.

## Doctor visit five

Next, I gave the A & E department at Stafford General Hospital a try. I knew this was going to take several hours before I was seen, but I needed some help.

I told the 'doctor' the dose of Amitriptyline I was on and that the dose had been increased from ten milligrams to one hundred and fifty milligrams. The increased dose had done nothing. The throbbing in my head was almost constant now. I practically begged him for help as I hadn't been offered any. He did the same coordination tests as the first 'doctor' and I had no difficulty performing them again. He then looked into my eyes with one of those lights on a stick (sorry if I'm being too technical), this allowed him to see inside the eyes. He found nothing and categorically told me there wasn't anything serious like a tumour, as he'd be able to see something. He sent me home without further medication and didn't refer me for any further investigation.

On Saturday third November 2007, two of my friends had a bonfire party. We were all in the back garden letting off fireworks, but I wasn't drinking as I was on Amitriptyline and I didn't feel at my best. Everybody was chatting, drinking and laughing but I was finding that repeatedly turning my head to look at the person talking was causing my head to throb. I was trying to join in with the fun and watch the fireworks as they flew up, but every time I looked up my head would throb again. Instead of sharing this with anybody I kept it to myself and again chose to avoid the problem by simply not looking up. I left at about midnight and went straight to bed.

The next morning Laura went to the bathroom. I got out of bed and forgot my routine of sitting on the side of the bed until the drums in my head finished their solo. I went straight from lying down to standing, walked a couple of steps and woke up on the floor to the sound of my name being shouted at me. I don't remember feeling any discomfort before passing out, my body just switched off when there was too much pressure on my brain. My parents lived around the corner and Laura phoned and asked them to come over. My Dad wouldn't listen to my attempts at playing the incident down, phoned the emergency doctor and demanded something was done.

## Doctor visit six

It was a Sunday, so I was sent to the on-call doctor at Stafford General Hospital. I explained the debacle so far and the head pains I'd been experiencing for months and their continual worsening. She told me to go to the doctor's, demand an MRI scan and not leave until I got one.

## Doctor visit seven

This was the first time I'd seen my preferred doctor. I hadn't seen her so far, simply because I wanted to see somebody straight away and it was a bit of a wait to see her.

She did the same coordination tests I had done twice before. I passed easily again this time. However, considering the increasing pain I'd been experiencing, she referred me for an emergency MRI scan to be sure there was nothing she couldn't see.

Hallelujah! Finally, some help!

My doctor read in my notes that a previous 'doctor' was going to refer me to a neurologist or for an MRI scan whichever came first. She was appalled to learn he did neither and went on holiday. That 'doctor' was no longer with the practice when I first blogged about this in 2010. I would say he was in his early forties in 2007, so he'll only be mid to late fifties now. I assume he's moved on to pastures new to get his large salary. I hope his incompetence was a one-off and somebody else hasn't paid for his mistakes. I consider him a major contributor to my condition; if he'd actually done what he said instead of swanning off on holiday, things might have been different. From my experience, he shouldn't be practising any more.

If he reads this he probably won't even realise I'm talking about him.

That was a Monday and the emergency MRI scan was for Thursday (a three-day wait doesn't seem like an emergency to me). That evening I had intense pain in my head and I was feeling sick. I was at my parents' house waiting for my girlfriend to get home from work, so I went upstairs, turned all the lights off and walked backwards and forwards from one bedroom at the end of the landing to the bedroom at the other. This was about five in the evening in November so without lights it was very dark. It didn't help, but it was the best I could think of, much like my brilliant idea of drinking Red Bull directly before having a nap.

Obviously this was a cure for a brain tumour that medical science didn't know of!

The next day I went round to my parents' again with the pain in my head. It was pretty constant now; it wasn't predictable any more, anything would set it off. Again I went upstairs to walk around in darkness across the landing. I felt sick, but it felt like I would *be* sick this time. As I was upstairs anyway doing my 'walking in a circuit' routine and next to the bathroom, I went in to throw up. I didn't, but the pain from retching was unbearable, it felt like my brain was trying to come out through my eye sockets. The throbbing in my head increased with each retch to the point I felt I was going to pass out. In fact I remember hoping I *would* pass out to stop the pain. Mum and Dad, hearing I was in distress, came upstairs and found me in tears on the floor next to the toilet. The pain had been unbearable, but it had subsided now that the retching had stopped. My head felt cloudy though and my vision seemed worse. It wasn't blurry, but it didn't seem clear either. This episode had scared the life out of me, but I still had a few days to wait until my emergency MRI.

The next night my girlfriend and I were watching Se7en in bed. I spent the entire film lying down with a flannel on my forehead looking up at the ceiling and listening as looking at the screen would start the pain again. I was worried now that the pain might make me retch again. We went to bed when the film finished, but the pain in my head told me I wasn't going to be able to sleep. I got up and went downstairs to watch a recorded *Top Gear*. The thumping in my head now felt that if I looked in the mirror I would see something pushing against my skull trying to get free. I started walking in a circuit around my living room and through the kitchen. Once again it didn't have any significant effect, but the pain did subside enough for me to go to bed about three hours later. And what had I been doing in those three hours? Yup, you guessed it, curing a brain tumour by walking for three hours!

The 'experts' would say I didn't complain of the typical symptoms other brain tumour sufferers do. This is true, I was able to sleep and lie down (typically the throbbing is worse when you lie down), I passed the coordination test three times with flying colours and the 'doctor' at A & E wasn't able to see anything inside my eyes with one of those lights on a stick (sorry, I'm being technical again).

My argument is this: I only had to see my own doctor once to get an MRI scan. She conducted the same coordination test, which I passed again with ease, but she still thought it best to get an MRI scan. The other 'doctor's' offered no help.

It was about one month (or maybe just under) between my first visit post-holiday and the scheduling of proper investigation by MRI. This is apparently within an acceptable time frame according to NHS rules. More on that later.

I should be dead now, only by a lucky series of events am I alive. There is nothing to say if the tumour had been identified earlier, my physical state would be any different. I should have had the opportunity to find out though.

The powers that be aren't to blame, but they are at fault.

# *Chapter 2*
# *George Michael, It Has A Name and Going Private*

### An Idiot Doing Idiotic Things

Let's go back even further.

The year is 2001 and I've just passed my driving test. I was so certain I was going to pass my test and - as previously stated - I wanted everything *now*, so I bought a brand new 1.2 Renault Clio that I would pick up a few hours after passing my test. And I did.

Six days later I was turning left into work, which had an incredibly narrow entrance. You had to swing out into the oncoming traffic so that your car was more or less straight when going through it. On the morning in question the string of oncoming cars was endless and I got bored with waiting, so naturally I rushed. I saw a small gap in the oncoming traffic and so took a smaller swing.

CRUNCH

The sound of bodywork on stone made me jump, but didn't make me stop, so I carried on through the entrance. The crunch became a scrape as the stone had already pressed against the front left door and was now scraping onto the rear left side.

I got out of the car and went straight into work and lay my head into my folded arms on my desk. I relayed what I'd done and what I already knew was confirmed for me. Somebody had gone and looked at the car and confirmed that both left side panels were heavily scratched and dented.

That stupidity cost £1500 pounds, paid for by the insurance meaning I had rather expensive insurance premiums for the next few years.

# Back in Reality

The MRI scan was at Cannock Chase Hospital in Cannock. I remember I was blissfully unaware of what was in store for me. Putting everything in writing and reading it back, it's fairly obvious. Although in my defence, I'm not sure it was obvious at the time. Things hadn't been unbearable for quite a long period, it became quite bad during the holiday in Turkey and the time after the holiday was miserable, but the months before that weren't too bad.

OK, only an idiot wouldn't have an idea of what was in store, but hey I'm an idiot! I had been told by four different 'doctor's' it wasn't serious after all. I'd even been told by one 'doctor' that it definitely **wasn't** a tumour.

I was replying to some emails for work before I left for the scan. I turned off the computer and got into the car. I didn't have any nervousness regarding what I was about to endure, I was quite naive and never gave any thought to what was about to happen. Nowadays I'd be worrying about all types of things: what if I feel sick in the tube/scanner/machiney thing but can't get out? What if I'm claustrophobic? (I'm not and never have been). I'd be certain they were going to find brain cancer and it would be terminal. What if we have a crash on the motorway on the way? What if we get stuck and I can't get out to go to the loo? What if we break down and we're stuck in the car and there's a sudden blizzard and the temperature drops, should I bring a coat? Maybe a hat and gloves? Has my phone got enough charge? What if we break down on a 'smart' motorway and there's no hard shoulder and we have to stop in the middle of the motorway and other motorists crash into us?

I used to see my naivety/stupidity as quite inconvenient. I'm now quite grateful as it helped me get through these difficult moments by not obsessing about what was wrong with me.

Laura drove me and my Mum to Cannock Chase Hospital. I got directions from a route planner on the Internet. The traffic was clear and it was a quick journey, despite my not being able to follow the simple directions. One of my major faults is believing I'm a lot better at something than I actually am and not admitting when I'm wrong or accepting help. The directions probably said something like 'turn left and take ___ road'. I insisted it was wrong and we should ignore it. As a result the journey was more complicated than it needed to be.

I used to get lost just backing out of the driveway.

We got to the MRI building about fifteen minutes early. I was handed a form with about ten or so yes/no questions. I filled it out, answering no to all of them. I don't believe I read the whole of the question as I was used to answering no to every question in those days. Nothing had ever happened to me, I wasn't allergic to anything and I was pretty sure I wasn't pregnant. I handed the form back to the receptionist and waited till I was called in.

The doctor who'd perform the scan came in, asked me if I had any metal objects on my person, told my Mum and my girlfriend how long the scan would be and to wait in the waiting room. I had to get on to a sort of tray that slid me inside a tube, I was given some earplugs and headphones. I put them on, but all I could hear was what sounded like a 56k modem dialling up.[2] The 56k modem did drown out the awful panpipe music though. My head was secured by a contraption designed to prevent any head movement but not cause any discomfort). I was given a small switch about the size and shape of a lipstick with a button you can press if the confinement is causing panic. Fortunately I didn't have any panic though. Half way through the scan the machine stopped making a noise, meaning I could now hear the music clearly. I remember praying for the machine to start again to drown it out. A nurse came in to give me an injection in my arm which introduces dye around the brain so it's more visible in the X-ray. The machine started up and thankfully the 56k modem drowned out the 'music' again.

This whole process wasn't going to reveal anything as far as I was concerned, it was just something I had to go through to eliminate anything serious. A panpipe rendition of a George Michael song was playing at the end of the scan. George put his panpipes down and a nurse slid me out of the tube. I was about to unleash a quip about the 'music' but the doctor spoke first.

"We've found something" The doctor said in a soft and sympathetic tone from a chair in the corner of the room.

I didn't react, I heard the words, but it was almost like an out of body experience. I didn't know how to react, should I burst into tears? I thought of the times I'd seen a situation

---

[2] If you're under forty and you don't know what I mean, then good. That's what you get for being young!

like this in a television drama and the person receiving the news usually had some sort of reaction, but I didn't know how to react. All I could think was 'they must think I'm some sort of robot'. I even contemplated reacting the way I thought they would have expected. We all have different ways though, there is no right or wrong way.

I hadn't made the connection or thought about how serious it was. The doctor hadn't confirmed what it was, but I knew that whatever had been spotted would need to be removed. I didn't think about how it would be removed, if it could be removed, if it was cancerous or not etc.

The doctor told me an ambulance would be there in a few minutes to take me to Stafford Hospital and Laura and Mum were waiting outside the room. They had already been told while I was still having the MRI scan. It had shown up at the start of the second half of the scan, it was a nervous fifteen-minute wait to see if the doctor would return with more bad news. My girlfriend was very upset and my Mum's eyes were very watery but she never cries out loud, it's always a very private affair, so much so it's difficult to notice unless you are looking at her.

Dad was in London for a meeting; he was on his way back as soon as he was phoned. The ambulance crew arrived to take me to Stafford Hospital. I had to sit in a chair to be transported to the ambulance, even though I could walk,

I was quite offended by this and said "It's ok I can walk."

"I know," she replied sympathetically. "But we have to transfer you on the chair."

I hadn't suddenly lost the ability to walk but I presume people getting this sort of news might be quite unsteady on their feet.

I'd never been in an ambulance before. Mum sat beside the bed and Laura sat in the chair behind my head and the non-driving member of the ambulance crew sat in the back as well. The driver said she was going to put the blue lights on as there would be a lot of school traffic. The reality hit me and I broke down. I'm in the back of an ambulance with the siren on.

All I could think about was how long I'd had this pain. I tried to think back to when I'd first noticed something wasn't right. My breathing problems? But that wasn't long ago. Sleeping every night with the fan on? That was months ago, but was it related? Maybe I was just hot. The breathing problems? The unbearable head pains?

Whatever it had been, I now knew I was in real trouble.

The ambulance pulled up outside A & E and I was taken out of the ambulance. I wanted to sit up to show that I wasn't ill, but I preferred a low sense of gravity in case we hit a pothole or something. I was taken through an entrance for patients who can't just walk into A & E. It never occurred to me that patients transported in an ambulance had to go through a different entrance, but it's not something I'd given any thought to in the past. I had to wait to be checked in with some other patients. Two male paramedics came in and stood behind me, one said to the other "that's the lad with the brain tumour". That really sent me into a panic, I thought to myself not only did I not know it was a brain tumour, but it was obviously not a common occurrence and my paramedic crew had been telling other paramedic crews.

As far as I was concerned this was the end.

My failure to react in the MRI room seemed to be because I didn't know what I was reacting to. Now I knew, and I was thinking 'I've left it for too long; I should have got the ball rolling on identifying this months ago. There's no coming back from this. I wasn't aware you could survive a brain tumour. I didn't know anyone who'd had one and I couldn't think of a story in the media about somebody surviving one. There are of course lots of survival stories and as technology and research is getting better, these success stories are becoming more frequent, but at that moment I wasn't thinking positively.

I was terrified, seeing what I call the 'behind-the-scenes' of A & E proved to me my demise was imminent. They don't show the backstage to most people, I must be special.

I was taken into a room, separated from other patients by a curtain, and left there to wait for a doctor to tell me how much longer I had left to live. The mood was very sombre, hardly any words were exchanged between us. I was thinking negative thoughts mainly about dying and things I wish I'd done differently. That led me to have a little weep on several occasions. After the longest forty-five minutes of my life a doctor came to see me.

'Here he is,' I thought, 'Dr Death, here to tell me how long I've got left to live.'

He did, indeed, bring bad news, though not what I'd expected. "The X-rays have been left in Cannock, we've sent a taxi to bring them back."

'What really?' I thought. 'There were two things to remember, the patient and the X-rays!'

We were waiting so long for the scans to arrive that Dad had arrived at the hospital after driving up from London. When they eventually arrived, the doctor confirmed I had a brain tumour. That hit me like a bus and I just looked at the floor and cried. This was the first time I'd heard it confirmed; I was still holding on to the idea that the paramedics were wrong, but now I knew they weren't. He said that they (Stafford Hospital) aren't the experts and they needed to talk to the neurosurgeons at North Staffs in Stoke-On-Trent.

It was early evening now so it was recommended I spend the night at Stafford on the A & E ward and they would consult with North Staffs and tell me the plan in the morning.

I didn't sleep at all that night. When you can't sleep, the night seems to drag, but when you do finally get to sleep your alarm seems to go off far too early. But when you can't sleep because you're wondering how long you've got left to live, time really drags, and you're as likely to nod off if you've just had a pot of coffee.

In this case I'm not sure if time dragging is a good or bad thing; is it better to delay the inevitable or get it over and done with?

The pain in my head was back. As I couldn't sleep I went exploring to try and take my mind off things. One of the nurses asked me if everything was alright, I explained I was fine, I couldn't sleep and I was going for a walk.

The fact that she had to ask was baffling. I had a brain tumour. Surely she knew I was going for the anti-brain tumour miracle walk. What do they teach in medical school?

I found a lounge. There was a coffee machine, a large plastic plant, some arm chairs and a table. There was a poster on the wall for Headway, a brain injury charity. I glanced over at it but didn't really take it in.

I sat down. The pain in my head had subsided, allowing me to reflect on the events of the day. Leaning forward with my head in my hands and my elbows resting on my legs, I broke down again.

Sitting on my own, undisturbed and undistracted, my mind was allowed to wander. I imagined a scenario where I ended up dead. Very few people knew of the symptoms I was having or for how long as I hadn't told people. It would be a bolt from the blue to them. I pulled my thoughts back. I wanted to stay positive; imaginations like this weren't going to help me. Within seconds my mind wandered to the worst scenario. I pulled it back again. For the third time it wandered off.

I needed to get my mind off it, so what did I do? I resumed the anti-brain tumour miracle walk. It didn't help this time either. My mind was still able to wander off, but at least I was getting some exercise.

A headache is usually a continuous pain, often located around the forehead. They are generally manageable and can be got rid of with a tablet or two.

My pain wasn't like this. Actions like looking up could trigger it. The world would move in slow motion. It felt like my skull wasn't big enough to contain my brain and it was banging against my skull.

If you're experiencing something similar, there's probably nothing serious going on. Don't panic, but don't ignore it either. Get proper medical advice and insist on a scan.

Don't let your doctor tell you there's nothing to worry about just because you aren't showing the classic symptoms. They can't tell you with certainty it's not a brain tumour without being able to see inside your head. Brain tumours kill more children and adults under the age of forty than any other cancer.

Steroids were prescribed to reduce the swelling of the tumour and reduce the pressure on my brain. They worked a treat; for the first time in months, I was pain-free.

I'm not sure what time a nurse came to see me in the morning. She informed me I would be transferred to North Staffs later that day to undergo surgery.

"Surgery?" The word sent me into a blind panic again.

Somehow it hadn't occurred to me that it's customary to remove a brain tumour. I told her that I'd had only a brief chat with a doctor who'd told me he needed to speak to the neurosurgeons at North Staffs. I'd learned I had a tumour by overhearing paramedics' gossip. Now I'd been told about brain surgery like the nurse was confirming something I already knew.

I phoned Dad's mobile, relayed what I'd been told, and he said they would be on their way in a few minutes. It's only a short distance from my parents' house to the hospital but with the adventure of finding a parking space they would probably be about thirty to thirty-five minutes. I was sitting on the bed watching the clock on the TV edge annoyingly slowly along. It was a digital clock and I watched the minute change and waited hours for it to change again.

When they finally arrived, they were tasked with the job of cheering somebody up who'd just been told they would be having brain surgery. I don't remember what was said; I'm sure there was a positive undertone to what was said, but seriously? How can you put a positive spin on this?

"Cheer up, at least you won't have head pains any more."

We were allowed to go into a side room and wait for a doctor to tell us the plan.

The doctor came in and confirmed again that it was a brain tumour.

'Fiddlesticks,' I thought (I'll let your imagination replace that word with a more appropriate one).

A small part of me had still hoped the doctor was going to say "Whoops! Sorry we got it wrong. It was just a headache after all." She would tut and say with a smile, "What are we like eh?"

She didn't. Her mood was very sombre as she told us that I would be transferred to North Staffs later that day. They would perform the operation and then I would spend the next twenty-four hours in ICU. I wondered if this meant that I'd be unconscious, awake but in pain, if my head would be shaved, if I'd have a wound; I knew nothing but it didn't occur to me to ask.

The doctor was careful not to offer an opinion on the diagnosis as she wasn't the expert. She said that the nurse wanted me to know she was very sorry for breaking the news the way she did; she was devastated and thought I knew more than I did.

I was transported to the ambulance on a bed, just as my brother Adam and his son Sam arrived. I told Adam what was happening without letting Sam know the details. I'm not sure how successful this was as he'd come to a hospital and seen me being wheeled away.

Into an ambulance again, this time with the siren turned off.

The same paramedics that brought me to Stafford were going to take me to North Staffs. We assumed our previous positions in the ambulance while Dad drove there via my house to pack some clothes and toiletries.

The trip was largely done in silence. I only remember two things about this trip, we got to North Staffs incredibly quickly and I had a little weep to myself.

I'm not sure what time we arrived but there wasn't much visiting time left, I was promptly shown to my bed in a very empty ward. My eldest brother Daniel didn't have to do much searching when he came to join us. He was fully aware of what was happening, but I decided to fill him in on the details anyway. I didn't get very far into telling him about my adventures because as soon as I mentioned the words "we've found something", I had another little cry.

I said earlier that I didn't know how to react, and should I burst into tears? It seems like I've answered that question. I didn't have to think about how I *should* react, because I couldn't help *but* react.

The neurosurgeon's assistant came to see me. He gave me some generic information about brain tumours, but I still hadn't spoken to the neurosurgeon so he limited himself in what he said about my case. It was probably for the best as what he did tell me went in one ear and out of the other. I did retain what he said about my recovery though. He said I would likely need physio to learn how to walk again as the tumour was on the cerebellum which amongst other things is responsible for one's balance.

My mind went into overdrive: if I've forgotten how to walk, what else will I have forgotten? Could I lose my memories? I might die in the operation. What if they think they've put me to sleep, but they haven't and I can feel everything?

Time for another little weep. A few days ago I was at home and now I'm in hospital listening to a doctor explaining what will happen when I have brain surgery. Brain surgery! I couldn't get my head around that (literally). The idea of someone opening my skull and removing things was terrifying. How can anybody know their way around a brain?

At no point had anyone suggested that I might not survive this. This doctor was just telling me I would need physiotherapy, something not needed by that many dead people. But the Doctor was talking about recovery - he could have been giving far worse news. The fact that I'd no longer be in constant pain should have encouraged me, but it didn't. I wasn't focusing on the outcome, I feared the means of getting there.

Visiting was over so we decided to go into the break room. The ward sister wasn't happy with this and told me visiting was over. I told her the news I had just received and that we'd only just arrived. She was sympathetic and said that was fine as long as we kept the noise down. Dad had brought a small portable DVD player and a selection of my DVDs, along with the recently released Hot Fuzz.

## It Has a Name

Mr Price, the neurosurgeon who would perform the operation, came in and explained what would happen. He brought the scans from the MRI with him and I was surprised by the clarity of the images. He explained the tumour was on the cerebellum which is at the back and bottom of the brain.

"This is away from the major clockwork," he said.

Mr Price explained that this was a haemangioblastoma.

"They're not malignant, and they usually shell out quite easily." For the first time I felt a glimmer of hope.

He told me I'd need about twelve weeks to recover fully. He didn't want to play down the importance of its removal, but this was a slow-growing, benign tumour that rarely caused lasting problems.

Haemangioblastoma grows in the blood vessels of the brain, spinal cord or retina. It isn't cancerous, but it may cause problems by growing and pressing on surrounding tissues. It needs to be removed because there's only so much room within the skull and most of it is taken up by the brain. If left it can become life threatening.

Within a few minutes of meeting him I was feeling more optimistic. Life wasn't going to end soon after all. I was still nervous; I had to undergo brain surgery, but many people go through surgeries in their life and in far more worrying circumstances.

I wasn't facing the possibility of death so I was much calmer now. I was happy for everyone to leave - Top Gear was about to start and Clarkson, Hammond and May could keep me company.

The reception was awful. I watched Top Gear as well as I could, but the picture was grainy and would often disappear at the top of the screen and reappear at the bottom like it was on a conveyor belt. I stayed in the break room for a short time afterwards, but there was nothing on and I returned to my bed to watch some of the DVDs Dad had brought. I watched *Hot Fuzz*, *The Life Of Brian* and *David Gilmour – Remember That Night*.

I didn't sleep at all that night. I should have been shattered, but the promise of brain surgery is a powerful stimulant. The neurosurgeon had made me feel a lot calmer about the situation, but the solution was still scary.

Early in the morning - I think about four - I asked the nurse for a sleeping tablet, but she couldn't as enough time hadn't passed since I'd received my steroid medication. The pain was gone, but I still couldn't sleep. Swings and roundabouts...

The next morning, I got straight out of bed and stood up without sitting on the side, ready for the throbbing to start. I didn't appreciate the magic of the steroids until I was showering in the wet room.

It was the first time I'd used a wet room. It was so big!

On my return the neurosurgeon was waiting at my bed.

"I'm afraid we've had to cancel today's surgery. There are no ICU beds available."

I did ask this time why I would need an ICU bed, and was told I would spend at least twenty-four hours there after surgery in case there were any complications. He told me the operation would be tomorrow morning now.

I have no memory of the rest of this day in hospital. I would imagine I watched some of the DVDs Dad had brought.

That night I got very little sleep again. I normally sleep quite well, but on the odd occasion I can't sleep I can put a podcast on at low volume and nod off to it. If that doesn't work, I can get my laptop out and watch Netflix or play Football Manager. I couldn't do that here though and as a result it was a long night. Time dragged. I resorted to trying to count sheep or singing through ninety-nine green bottles, knowing that I wasn't going to remain focused on either without my mind wandering off to a depressing place.

A guy had been brought into the bed next to me following a head injury operation. He had a shaved head. I didn't know if this was because of the operation or this was his hair style. My guess was the former as a shaved head didn't suit him. He had a large plaster on his head, and it was obviously covering his operation wound as I could see dried blood. When he was awake he would mutter to himself and shout for a nurse; the nurse would never come and he would soon nod off again and snore. I wasn't bothered by his snoring, there was no danger of me getting to sleep anyway and he seemed to be in some distress when he was awake, so sleeping was the best option for him.

His presence at least gave me something else to think about. I felt sorry for him, I wondered what he was like before and wondered how his family would cope now. Would he be permanently affected or was this just temporary?

'It must be temporary' I reasoned, 'you have to go to the ICU for at least twenty-four hours so it must be a good sign that he's back on the ward'. This was the only non-tumour thought I had all night. At least the day on a hospital ward starts quite early so I didn't have to try and sleep for much longer.

In the morning Mr Price informed me that the operation had been cancelled again because an ICU bed still wasn't available.

'This really isn't that serious to them,' I thought. 'I'm not a priority'.

I think this was a Tuesday and the operation had been rescheduled for Friday. Mr Price explained I could go home as there was no need to wait in the hospital. I would need to be back on Thursday evening. I asked him if it was safe to postpone it and he explained he wasn't too concerned as it is a slow-growing tumour in a non-critical location.

I was ready to leave the ward and go home but was unable to as there was some hold up with getting my steroid medication from the pharmacy. After many hours the lunch cart came around and, as I wasn't supposed to be here, there wasn't any lunch for me.

I asked the nurse if there was anything for me, but she didn't know who I was. I could choose from two unclaimed dishes - liver and onions and another dish which I can't remember. I hadn't had liver and onions before but from the selection I thought it was the best choice. The jury's still out on that.

Another thirty minutes went by, and Daniel arrived to take me home.

"I can't yet" I said.

"Why?" He responded.

"They haven't given me my medication."

After waiting for a while, he went to ask what the hold-up was and was told there wasn't a member of staff available to go and get my medication. He explained that I was in for brain surgery, my operation had been cancelled twice and I could spend a short time at home before I had to return to hospital; a short time that became even shorter the longer they took.

Well, would you believe it? Someone was able to go and get it and we were on our way a few minutes later.

## Going Private

When the tumour was first diagnosed, my uncle had kindly offered to pay for private treatment. I was entirely happy with the reassurances of the neurosurgeon, Mr Price, and Stoke-on-Trent was only twenty minutes from home, but the cancellations were becoming worrying. My 'routine' brain tumour wasn't urgent. It might not have been of vital importance to them, but it was of great importance to me.

I'd previously turned down my uncle's offer as it looked like I would have the operation quickly on the NHS, and I was assured it wasn't a case of life or death. My uncle thought it was important to get it out as soon as possible, regardless of what I'd been told. The offer was still there if I changed my mind.

I phoned him as soon as I got home and asked him if I could take him up on his offer. After much discussion we worked out a payment plan so that I could repay him and he grudgingly loaned me the money.

That's not entirely true – he'd said yes before I finished asking him.

I phoned my Grandad, who gave a very philosophical outlook on it. He was very sorry this had happened to me but concentrated on the positives. The diagnosis could have been a lot worse and even though having brain surgery seemed like a scary prognosis it's just the word 'brain' that's scary. Take that word out, he said, and it's much less worrying.

Next I phoned my Nan. She said she was praying for me and the priest was going to say mass for me tomorrow, and again on the day of the operation.

Remember I mentioned a lucky series of events? Well, here's the first bit of luck...

Daniel did some phoning around for me. Unbeknown to me at the time, he had spoken to my uncle before my taking up his offer of going private, and had already started the ball rolling on finding somebody to do the surgery. His first port of call was to ring the office of the neurosurgeon at North Staffs. He spoke to Mr Price's assistant surgeon, who highly recommended Professor Cruickshank at The Priory in Birmingham as he used to work with him. He gave Daniel the professor's number.

As luck would have it Professor Garth Cruickshank is at the forefront of neuroscience and in my opinion he is the **G**reatest**O**f**A**ll**T**ime. I don't want to miscredit him here, so I won't go into specifics - largely because I've just Googled him and there are several articles where every word is no less than seven syllables. I firmly believe that I would not be here if it wasn't for this brilliant man.

Daniel phoned me to tell me he'd found this surgeon. He had a really good feeling about him and urged me to have the operation done by him.

I was a bit wary of taking the offer; I'd always been taught never to take the first quote and to shop around. But this wasn't a quote for an exhaust, this was brain surgery and time was of the essence. I agreed to go with the Prof.

I'd been more than happy to have the operation on the NHS, but there was this other option open to me, and I just wanted the tumour out ASAP.

Being at home meant one thing: sleep! I felt as though sleep and I had some unfinished business.

That night we ordered a Chinese and watched *The Sopranos*. Well, 'watched' might be a bit misleading as I was shattered and saw very little. We called it an early night and I went to bed. Thanks to the steroids, I got up from the sofa without pain and got into bed without the need of a fan blowing cold air in my face. I went straight to sleep. Ah, bliss!

Morning arrived far too quickly, I wanted to sleep in but was rudely woken by my alarm chirping at me, reminding me to take some steroids. I contemplated trying to go back to sleep but I realised I could have another pain free shower. I remember thinking 'this is okay, I don't need an operation'.

That thought was only brief as I quickly came to the conclusion that it was a stupid idea. Adam came round and we played *Assassin's Creed* on the Xbox 360 that I'd bought a couple of days ago.

# Chapter 3
# *Tina Turner's Birthday, We Have a Problem and the ICU*

### An Idiot Doing Idiotic Things

My Dad and uncle were going to Arnold Clarke with my Grandad to get him a second-hand car.

'I like cars' I thought, 'I'll tag along'.

I was looking to buy a house and I thought, 'I can't afford a house and the car, therefore my pride and joy car needs to be downgraded.'

This was an instant decision and not something I'd thought about before. As I'd just suddenly decided this, I didn't give my girlfriend the chance to talk me out of this. I relied on my own council and, well, I'm an idiot.

Proud of myself for taking the grown-up decision of sacrificing the car to move onto the next stage of my life, I went car shopping.

We got to Arnold Clarke and a salesman told me the price I could get for mine in a part exchange. I can't remember the figure, but I'm sure they'd be offering about £3500 less than they would sell it for. I had a look around and there was virtually nothing I could swap for mine without paying extra. I'd come across a bottom-of-the-range Nissan Almera and a second-hand Vauxhall Astra. As this was 2005, the Astra was about four models before the current model on the road now. It didn't even have air conditioning or a CD player.

Note for younger people: A CD player was the cutting-edge technology we used back then to listen to music. Streaming wasn't an option because it didn't exist, smart phones were primitive and Bluetooth was a little-known Danish king.

Whatever, all the Astra had was a cassette player. Sorry, I forgot the younger generation again. A cassette player is…

So, the options:

1. Swap my Clio for a one-year-old Vauxhall Astra with no CD player or aircon.
2. Swap it for a new car with both, but little else other than the 'distinction' of being a Nissan.
3. Keep the Clio and investigate my options in more detail when I get home, as this didn't have to be done now.

It's obvious which of these any non-idiot would choose. This idiot chose option two.

I quickly agreed to swap my Clio for the Nissan. I shook hands with the salesman and he walked away, clicking his heels and laughing. I'd just swapped my imported two-litre dream car for a bottom-of-the-range Nissan Almera S.

I was instructed to come back on Friday to collect it as, apparently, they were going to need a few days to prepare the Nissan; I'm not sure what this meant.

That gave me five days to change my mind. I'm sure the salesman had told his colleagues, "I bet he phones before Friday and pulls out of the deal."

I didn't.

I drove the 172 to Arnold Clarke listening to my favourite CD, with the climate control blasting and tears in my eyes. On the way back I discovered that the Nissan's aircon felt like a small hamster blowing gently through a straw. I would have been more comfortable being dragged behind the car on my face. I was bawling like Ben Stiller at the end of *There's Something About Mary*. An old man on a mobility scooter looked at me sympathetically as he overtook me.

# Back in Reality

## My Dad took me to The Priory to have some blood taken, this was in case I contracted MRSA or some other hospital

superbug. This was a few years after MRSA had become a major issue. It wasn't as widespread at this time as it had been, but it was still a concern and it's always good to be prepared. I had to be at The Priory in Birmingham for the operation in three days.

The following days were quite pleasant - by pleasant I mean pain-free. The knowledge that I would have brain surgery in a few days did take a lot of the joy out of things. I don't remember doing much; family popped in, we may have spent an evening at my parents' house or Laura's parents' house. I do remember I went with my parents to help Adam move into a new house. I was feeling fine and insisted I could be of more use and lift heavy things but was reminded I'd got a brain tumour, given some coat hangers to carry and ordered away.

'What a waste' I thought. 'I'm on steroids, give me something heavy to shift.'

## November 26th 2007

A date that's forever etched in my memory. It's Tina Turner's birthday!

I checked into The Priory in Birmingham the evening before the operation. Mum, Dad and Laura came with me.

We were shown up to my room and after a short time I was presented with a menu for that evening's dinner. There were three choices, one of which was steak followed by some sort of tempting dessert. The alternative was to reject this sumptuous feast and accompany my guests and pay for the privilege of eating in the cafeteria.

Guess what I chose?

We went down to the cafeteria, which had already been open for a while. There wasn't much to choose from even if you're willing to eat meat, which Dad isn't. He's vegetarian. All he could have was a cold, chewy slice of pizza and some oven chips which seemed to have been out under the hot lamps for a while. I think I had a stale hot dog with the same mummified oven chips, accompanied by a drink from the vending machine. I could have put a window through with the hotdog roll; the chips had been part-cooked some time last week and supplied with life support by forty-watt bulbs.

'I should have had the steak' I thought.

We stayed in the cafeteria for about an hour and a half, chatting. It wasn't a solemn chat because as far as we knew there was nothing to be solemn about. I wasn't looking forward to having brain surgery tomorrow though, so it was a welcome distraction. We headed back up to the room at my request. It was before ten o'clock but I was completely shattered; not even the worry of brain surgery in the morning was going to keep me awake. The three of them left and would be back in the morning.

I decided to watch the television until I was tired enough to fall asleep. The room apparently had Sky television, but I had access to very few channels, including not all of the terrestrial channels. Not that it mattered, I only wanted it on to help me fall asleep. I didn't stay awake for long. It was an indication of how tired I was, or it could be because I wasn't worried sick about the outcome of my surgery the next day.

I was woken in the morning by Daniel, Adam, Mum, Dad and Laura. I slowly opened my eyes and saw five faces smiling down at me. Sorry, hang on, I forgot I wasn't in an episode of the Waltons. I was woken with the grace and decorum of a marching band clanging cymbals together.

The anaesthetist came a bit later to introduce himself, explain his role and tell me what was going to happen.

"It's a fairly quick operation. You should be back here in an hour or so."

He left and would return shortly to collect me and take me to the operating theatre. The anaesthetist left my room and the usual Shaw banter ensued. My mind was completely taken off the surgery. I was laughing without my head throbbing. I'd be able to do this without the need for steroids in the not-too-distant future. A joking prediction was made which ironically turned out to be a lot closer to the eventual reality than anybody thought was possible. None of us had contemplated any complications.

The anaesthetist arrived to take me to the operating theatre.

Gulp.

The laughing stopped and the reality of what was about to happen hit me. There was no taking the simple route now; the route I'd tried so many times before. This was the final roll of the dice.

I was adamant I didn't want to be pushed on a gurney. I wasn't hurt or injured, and I wanted to walk down. I was ready for some pushback, but I felt strongly about this.

"That's fine, we were going to walk down to the theatre anyway" the anaesthetist said.

"We'll see you in a couple of hours," I was told reassuringly "Good luck."

I didn't make any attempt at a funny reply as my usual ability to take nothing seriously had evaded me at this moment.

I walked to the operating theatre. I can't explain this feeling, I was incredibly nervous - scared is probably a more accurate description. I was putting on a brave face but inside I was bricking it. I told myself, 'This part is easy. I'll just have a nap and when I wake up it will all be over'.

There was no thought that this was anything but routine. The month leading up to this had been miserable, but when I woke up I'd be fixed.

The operating theatre was on the ground floor. It took about two minutes to get there.

I went through some double doors, followed by a security door and was asked to get onto a bed/trolley. I was in a side room next to the operating theatre which seemed to double up as a room to hold stock; cupboards were on the left with a work surface on top and a sink. There were other cupboards on the upper part of the wall.

Superman… Sorry, I mean Professor Cruickshank, was in here preparing for the operation. I can't imagine being in his shoes; it must take a special kind of person to specialise in brain surgery. It's complicated beyond contemplation when things go according to plan, but imagine when you're presented with something completely unexpected - as mine turned out to be.

I don't remember much about being anaesthetised. I do remember being asked to count to ten aloud.

"One…two…three…four…five…six…seven"

I remember thinking "this isn't working, I must be the only person they've met who's resis…" That's the last thing I remember. I lasted seven whole seconds.

Obviously I don't have a personal account of the operation so I can only relay what I've been told.

Mum, Dad and Laura waited for several hours. The operation was taking longer than predicted.

It was around six hours later when Professor Cruickshank returned.

"You've probably worked out that things aren't going to plan. The tumour has an abnormal blood supply, and this hospital isn't equipped for what we need to do."

I would be transferred to the Queen Elizabeth Hospital about a mile and a half away where he could bring in his full team and what we later learned was a unique piece of specialist equipment.

My parents and girlfriend drove to the Q.E. and waited in a shabby waiting room with slashed seats and a broken vending machine. Quite a contrast!

More hours crept by. Professor Cruickshank returned with horrific news.

"It's essentially inoperable. It's become entangled with several hundred tiny blood vessels. The big problem is that it's so distended with blood it's likely to burst at any point, almost certainly within the next forty-eight hours."

My father asked about the risk of operating.

"The risk of *not* operating is that he is unlikely to live more than two days."

The Prof explained that any of the blood vessels could be an essential supply to the brain stem. Every one he cut was likely to starve a part of the brain of oxygen, so he knew he was going to cause damage, but it was near-impossible to predict to what extent.

"There's a strong chance it will kill him."

Faced with the choice of virtually assured death or a slim chance of survival, Mum and Dad made the obvious – but impossibly difficult – choice.

Professor Cruickshank put on his Superman cape and got to work.

After thirteen hours, Professor Cruickshank came back.

"Well, it's out, and I'm an older man for it. He's survived the operation, but the next twenty-four hours will be critical."

Part of the rear part of my skull had been removed to gain access. As is apparently normal, it wasn't replaced, meaning there is a dip at the back of my head just above the top of my neck, along with an inch-long scar. Neither are visible currently due to my rapidly diminishing hair growth.

It's since been said to my father by other doctors and surgeons that the Prof was possibly the only neurosurgeon in Britain who could have performed the operation with such success.

So there you have it; three bits of incredible luck:

1. My uncle paying for me to go private.
2. Daniel finding Professor Cruickshank to do the operation. I don't believe there's anyone else in the

world who could have kept me alive and given me the quality of life I do have.
3. The cancellations of my operation at Stoke put me less than two miles from one of only two neurology machines capable of saving my life. The other was in Edinburgh.

\*\*\*

I've asked my Dad to write his account of my time in the ICU. I was otherwise engaged at this point and my account probably wouldn't make for great reading.

The atmosphere of the Critical Care Unit at Queen Elizabeth Hospital is slightly unreal. Each bed houses a comatose shape, surrounded by bleeping technology and – initially unaccountably – an assortment of cheap fans direct from the Argos catalogue. Shell-shocked relatives move silently through the tangled cables. Chance meetings have the politeness of a funeral party.

We found Tom next to a man who'd attempted suicide by jumping off a road bridge. Though comatose, he repeatedly groaned and clutched his genitalia. Opposite was a young girl with head injuries from a car crash. In the middle of all this tragedy was Tom; the guy who'd walked confidently out of the ward that morning. Like all his ward-mates, he was the nexus of a spaghetti of wires, tubes and drains. A hand-written note taped to his head bore the chilling message: "No bone".

The next few days were a terrifying roller-coaster ride. Initially, things looked encouraging: "He's awake," said a nurse, "You can get him to squeeze your hand."

It worked! Encouraged, we suggested "one squeeze for yes, two for no". That level of communication was too complex for now, but that tiny twitch of returned pressure told us that Tom was still in residence.

Then the fits started.

The first came within 48 hours. A call from the hospital panicked us; the nurse explained that Tom had "begun fitting" in the early hours of the morning. The fits became more regular, and a change in medication to reduce them sank Tom deep into unconsciousness. The tenuous hand-squeezing link was broken.

Over the following days, the attempted suicide began to improve; the prognosis for full recovery was good. The young car-crash victim rallied strongly, and then died suddenly; fate plays inscrutable tricks.

As Tom's intra-cranial pressure dropped to more normal levels, he began once more to regain consciousness. On a good day the hand-squeezes almost constituted communication – one squeeze for "yes", no squeeze for either "no", or "I'm not here at the moment, please leave a message."

Day by day, Tom's bed moved further from the nurses' station as his condition became less parlous. It became ever more certain that he would survive. The question now was to what degree.

# *Chapter 4 - Kelly Crabtree, Pacman Ghosts & Blue Chairs*

Around a month passed by before things were happening that I can sort of remember. For example, I know I was in hospital for Christmas '07 but I have no memory of it.[3]

I have a few confused, fragmented memories. Some of them make enough sense to appear in the main story, but there are a few I can't attribute to any timeline. Most of them didn't happen at all, but they're in my memory banks as reality.

## Fragmented Memories

I've been kidnapped, along with two other lads. Our hands are tied behind our backs and our feet are bound at the ankles. We're all sitting in the back of a white Ford Transit van, hands behind our backs and legs bent at the knees. I know the colour and make because my vision swooped from outside the van to the inside, like a camera on a drone. The director of this movie obviously felt we had to show the Ford badge, like it was an important bit of product placement.

I don't remember the actual kidnapping. I think the vision started with us tied up in the van.

---

[3] Well that's the story I'm sticking to anyway, as it got me out of buying presents that year.

I don't know what happened to the van, because the vision then changed to us, still tied up, but now in a derelict building. It was formerly the Reynold's Club, a bar that used to exist on the outskirts of Stafford. There was nothing much around it, just a KFC and a Halfords.

We were on the first floor and there was a very large window spanning the whole width of the wall. There was no communication between us captives, but I remember a feeling of panic, like I wanted to get away.

The scene then changed again, and now I was in a private room in hospital and Daniel was there. I told him I'd been having terrible dreams and showed him a pot of chocolate mousse the nurses had left me because of my bad night.

## Another Fragmented Memory

The kidnapping theme continues. I'm sitting on the bow of a boat with my hands tied behind my back and my legs bent at the knees in front of me. It was like Tony Soprano's boat, not very big and you get to the bridge by climbing a ladder. Above me are the actor who played Jango Fett in Star Wars: Attack of the Clones, and the actress who played Kelly Crabtree in Coronation Street. Both are standing on the bridge, staring into the distance as though they're posing for a calendar.

## Another Fragmented Memory

I'm in a room that's very wide but quite narrow. As you enter, there's only a couple of meters before you reach the opposite wall. It's brick below a wide glass window that extends the full length of the room. I'm lying on a mattress and I'm the only person in the room.

This time there's no feeling of panic or sense that I'm being held against my will, but I still don't appear to be moving. I don't know if this is because I can't or just choose not to. I can only assume it's the latter.

Outside, there's an expanse of grass and some tall buildings. They look like the skyline of New York if you were looking inland from some way out in the harbour. Two figures are running along the rooftops, leaping between buildings like Parkour athletes. They're like the small, undetailed sprites that you'd see on 1980s computer games. They're leaping between buildings and keep me entertained for hours. I can't tell you if they just keep running along an endless New York skyline or if they keep re-appearing at the start, like a character that's lost a life in a computer game.

## Back in Reality

Regaining consciousness was going to be the first indication of how brain damaged I was. Had Professor Cruickshank cut any blood vessels that were essential to the brain stem? The hand-squeezing while I was in ICU had been encouraging progress, but was merely a sign of brain activity.

I awoke in a ward in the Queen Elizabeth hospital in Birmingham. I wasn't wondering where I was or what had happened. I didn't think 'hang on the original prognosis was six weeks recovery and some physio leading to a full recovery'. I didn't have any memory of the original prognosis. I didn't fight to get out of bed and walk. I didn't have a sudden panic, noticing drips connected to my body and attempt to pull them out.

When I say I awoke, it didn't happen like the flick of a switch. My memories are fragmented (see above), but I'm told that some days I'd be aware and others a zombie, frozen and unable even to blink. This isn't uncommon with brain injury; recovery doesn't happen in straight lines, and everyone is different.

What follows is my attempt to make sense of this.

I didn't look up at the smiling faces around me, and I didn't say "er…hello?". In fact I didn't say anything at all. I'd been given a tracheostomy after the operation to help me breathe. This is a small operation in which a hole is opened into the trachea. A tee-shaped device called, for some reason, a Swedish nose is inserted. This has a filter to keep debris out, and it significantly reduces the effort required to breathe.

There is, however, a downside. The drier, colder air you're breathing increases mucus output. This can be serious as it's possible for the tube to become blocked and suffocate the patient. The solution is to remove the Swedish nose and insert a flexible plastic rod to provoke coughing. This isn't pleasant, even if you're semi-comatose.[4]

I was being sustained through a naso-gastric tube. This can also have unpleasant side-effects.

---

[4] It's not that pleasant for the person doing it either, who can find themselves on the receiving end of a high velocity wad of yellow nastiness.

I was on my back, with a slack jaw that left my mouth permanently open. With no food to process, this presented ideal conditions for fungus growth.

I developed an extravagant thrush infection that meant sheets of grey blotting paper needed regular excavation.

Waking up presented the first opportunity to use my eyes. They'd been tested while I was unconscious to check the pupils were reacting to light. My eyes had been open, unfocused and apparently pointing in the same direction.

What's clear now is that my right eye was misaligned. It's normal for your eyes to turn inwards as an object gets closer, with both refocusing as needed.

My eyes were out of sync. As something came closer, one eye – it could be either – would begin to move inwards while the other looked straight ahead. Then the other would take over, flick inwards while the first eye moved back to centre.

I had double vision and everything was blurred.

At the time I didn't think this was abnormal. I was lying immobile in a bed, receiving signals from my eyes. It just didn't occur to me to question any of it. I was conscious, but things just *were*; I wasn't processing any of the information received.

I'll hand over to Dad to fill in some blanks.

**These were difficult days. We'd been told that recovery from a brain injury isn't linear, but seeing days of progress suddenly vanish was devastating. On a good day, Tom would respond with slight nods or shakes of the head and we'd be able to communicate, albeit at a low**

level. His temperature was erratic, often soaring to dangerous levels. Although the early post-op fits had subsided, sometimes a temperature spike would induce a recurrence. Most occurred at night when we weren't there, but we were there to witness one of them. Outwardly, there wasn't much to indicate what was happening; slight trembling in the arms and tightening of the jaw were the only clues. But Tom usually didn't move at all, so we were alert to the slightest change.

We called the nurse. "He's fitting," she said immediately and brought extra fans.

The following day we found Tom under what appeared to be an over-inflated sleeping bag. This was a chambered quilt into which cooled air was blown constantly. To us, the temperature inside felt arctic, but there were no more fits.

This added to the technology surrounding Tom. He was already equipped with a space-age mattress that constantly changed the pressure in various parts of the bed to prevent pressure sores. Sustenance was delivered by tubes, oxygen was connected as necessary, and wires were connected to every conceivable body part for analysis by the bank of screens next to the bed. The soundtrack came from an assortment of reassuring bleeps and alarming sirens. The arrangement of the devices changed regularly, and some days our visits were to a distant and barely visible figure.

Tom's responsiveness varied considerably, but we became increasingly concerned that the trend seemed to be negative. Over a week or so, he withdrew completely, apparently unaware of our presence.

My bed was in a room directly opposite the nurses' station. My memory is that the room was quite large, shared with many other people. I'm not sure why I thought this as I didn't see anything apart from the ceiling.

I've been back since my stay here and it's completely different from my vague memories. It is quite a small room and only has four beds.

The limitations of yes/no communication become clear when your visitors don't know what you want. They'd try to guess, usually incorrectly.

"Are you too hot?" Shake of the head.
"Too cold?" Shake of the head.
"Do you want the TV on?"
...and so on.

The real nightmare was when I had an itch that needed urgent scratching. The request to attend to a troublesome itch was significantly more difficult than other requests, as once they'd determined the requirement, they would then have to find out where the itch was.

At first I could barely roll my eyes in disgust at their stupidity, but slowly I regained some movement in my arms. My hands were barely mobile, but I could raise my arms and point in the general direction of something.

My hands were pointing down at an almost ninety-degree angle from my wrist. I didn't know this was an unnatural position and it hadn't been mentioned by the doctors, so I had no desire to try and move them.

This did, however, make it difficult to understand what I was pointing at, especially if I pointed at the wrong image of my double vision.

Usually I was too hot or too cold. A fan was supplied so that I could turn it on and off without repeatedly asking somebody to do it. It had a big red button, like a switch you would see in a comedy underneath a label that says "do not press". The size of it was a necessity due to my wayward right arm. It would wave around, refusing to take the direct route to its destination. I'd notice the arm veering right and move it left, but I'd over-correct, so it would veer left, and I would try and correct by moving it right again. This is what's known to motor cyclists as a tank slapper. When it finally landed near the intended destination, I struggled to muster the required force to push the button.

I would push the button with my knuckles and be satisfied by the change in temperature for a few minutes, before pressing the switch again. I'd sometimes repeat this process several times in a minute.

There were two visiting times each day, two till four pm and six till eight pm. Mum, Dad and Laura would come to both every day. As the hospital is about forty minutes from where they live, they would go and get some dinner and come back for the second visiting period. I don't remember experiencing depression or sadness as the time for them to leave approached. I don't think I would have been aware of the time and the first time I knew of their departure was just before they left.

I slept a lot at this time anyway, I imagine the concoction of drugs I was on meant I didn't have much of a say in this. I was often asleep when they arrived, I was in and out of slumber the whole time they were there.

I had a catheter. I don't know this for sure as I've never asked anybody but that's because I'm fairly sure the answer has got to be yes. It's not something I need to know, I'm more than happy just assuming this. I have a vague memory of constantly complaining there was something 'not right' down there. I've put 'not right' in inverted commas which gives the impression I said it. I didn't. I'm sure banging on the bed for attention and then pointing at your groin while maintaining eye contact with your Mother would probably make her feel uncomfortable.

My method of getting people's attention was to bang on the bed, I think it was for things like turning the fan on/off. I have a vague memory of one of the nurses saying, "I'm coming Tom!" My incessant attention seeking must have been very annoying.

## Another Fragmented Memory

I was in a room made out of bed sheets, the floor was made of pillows and there was something affecting my mobility as movement seemed impossible.

There were floating objects that looked like puppets that you would find on *CBeebies* or the ghosts in *Pacman*.

There were other patients in here with me, trying to get out. Everybody eventually managed it, although the last person to leave was stuck with me for some time. There was no communication between us. The only sound was me shouting "This isn't fair!"

The other patient did finally get out and I began to panic. I was petrified because I was the only one left and I didn't know if there would be consequences.

Mum, Dad and Daniel then appeared in the ward, and the floating puppets and sheets disappeared.

# Back in Reality

Mum, Adam and Laura were allowed to take me outside in the small garden connected to one of the wards. I was given a wheelchair that offered a lot of support. The backrest looked as though it had cushions set into it, but I think they were just for show as it offered no comfort. The backrest was about the length of my torso and unadjustable, it was made of plastic or something similar and forced the patient to sit with a straight back. I found this quite uncomfortable as my back was being forced into the correct position which it hadn't been for a while.

On top of the backrest was a small metal bar attached to the back of a cushioned headrest.

This was quite a serious piece of kit, Great for somebody who couldn't sit upright without support and needed arm rests either side to stop them from tipping to the side.

I was given a scarf, a coat, a warm woolly beanie hat, some gloves and a throw to cover my legs. I looked like a little old woman feeding the pigeons in the park during winter.

It took about twenty minutes just to get ready for my adventure.

It was about a three-minute walk from the ward to the outside area. There was a pond with a small bridge over it and this was my first taste of the outdoors in weeks. I was fortunate to be able to experience this; I'd been close to death but now I was able to go out in the fresh air.

So you'd think my thoughts would be quite profound… nope! 'I'm cold!' I thought.

My feet weren't wrapped up like the rest of me and they quickly felt like ice blocks. This would have been December, which is not the coldest of months, but not exactly t-shirt weather either. Adam had only pushed me to the opposite side of the courtyard when I signalled I wanted to go back in. We were outside for about one minute.

## Blue Chair

Around this time I was introduced to the Dreaded Blue Chair.

My first experience would be the only time I would happily sit in it. I was polite, enthusiastic and blissfully unaware of what I was letting myself in for. Future occasions would require coercion, pleading and the threat of a Hannibal Lecter mask to stop me from biting.

You may be picturing the Iron Throne of Westeros, surrounded by mist and dry ice. It was actually a nice, comfortable chair, more like the armchairs that Joey buys in the second series of *Friends*. It was blue. It was comfy, It had padded arms and a padded back.

If you're thinking that this doesn't sound particularly torturous, you're wrong.

It was ever so slightly slippy.

Granted, an able-bodied person would have no issue sitting on it and staying put, but I'd spent weeks in bed and I *did* have difficulty. I almost immediately slid down the chair and would have ended up in a heap on the floor if I wasn't able to stop myself with my legs. Within seconds my head was resting against the bottom of the rear cushion, my back was on the seat cushion, and my feet were on the floor, trying to support me.

The nurse moved me back into the correct seating position and said "Try to use your feet on the floor to hold yourself up."

I pushed my feet hard against the floor and this time I held myself up, I held myself up for long enough that the nurse left me.

"There you go" she encouraged, "much better! You ok if I go over there?"

I nodded, but I wasn't comfortable. If I could talk, my answer would have been "I'd rather you didn't, I think I'm going to need you again in a few minutes."

With no means of communicating this, I just smiled and nodded.

It was taking a mighty effort not to slide and inevitably I got tired and slid down, preventing myself from falling in a heap on the floor by using my feet again. The nurse was on the other side of the room and had her back to me. I banged on the chair but quite softly. I didn't intend for it to be inaudible, but I couldn't put the required force into banging on the chair. It was as though I couldn't move my hand independently from my forearm.

Quite often I slid into a position that hurt my back. But I couldn't ask for help so I would bang on the chair to attract attention. After a few bangs on the arm of the chair, the nurse would come, but she had several other patients to look after, so I would be in this position for a while.

This happened several times. On each occasion I was able to keep myself up a bit longer, but simply because I withstood the burning from the lactic acid in my legs. I knew I was eventually going to give up and slide down, but I was challenging myself to sit for longer each time.

After lunch each day I'd be put into the activities room to endure an hour or so of torture.

It seemed longer. Fortunately, I couldn't talk, so my expletives were internal.

# *Chapter 5 - No Longer a Righty, Wall Pin and Stokeward Bound*

### An Idiot Doing Idiotic Things

Let me take you back to 2006.

I'm twenty-three and I'm about to drive my Dad to see David Gilmour at the Royal Albert Hall in London. The original plan was for him to drive us down in his much nicer car, but he decided to pick a fight with a tractor whilst riding his motorbike a few months earlier and lost.

One day I received an email saying David Gilmour would be touring his new album and members of his website had the chance to buy tickets a day before the rest of the public.

'Well, I only need one of my kidneys' I reasoned. I sold my least favourite one and bought two of the most expensive tickets.

I printed off a ticket, blacked out the price and put it inside a Christmas card and gave it to Dad for Christmas 2005.

Every year since, he's opened his Christmas card, immediately tipped it up and when nothing falls out says "not your best effort".

Unfortunately, his squabble with a tractor had put our intended attendance in doubt.

I phoned The Royal Albert Hall and asked them if I could change our booking to disabled seats.

"You could," came the reply. "Do you really want to though? The disabled seats are quite far back and up in one of the balconies. Your seats are front row."

"Front row, you say? He'll just have to learn to walk again then." I put the phone down and told him we were sticking with the original tickets. I think his response was "abso-bloody-lutely."

The day of the concert was very warm, but due to a previous bout of idiocy - selling my gorgeous Renault Clio 172 in favour of a Nissan Almera S - we were both sweltering.

The 'asthmatic hamster blowing through a straw' poor excuse for air con, wasn't keeping us cool.

"It's got electric windows that nearly always work", I boasted.

The noise from the car straining to hit seventy was deafening, so we put the windows up.

We got close to The Royal Albert Hall and I drove around looking for somewhere to park that was close to The Royal Albert Hall, so Dad wouldn't have to go too far on his crutches.

I drove around but couldn't find anywhere to park and without realising I turned into a road that took me towards Hyde Park.

I realised that I didn't know how to get out, but there was a car about one hundred yards in front of me, so I thought I'd follow it, and if it turns into the park, I'll just carry on past it.

A plan that required me to get closer to the car so as not to lose it. I didn't though and I couldn't see the car any more.

I should have realised that it had turned off because the road we were on was becoming a track, heading into Hyde Park.

"oops, I don't think we should be here." I admitted stating the obvious "I'll turn off at the first opportunity."

That opportunity never came and I followed the track until it ended, joining a wide tarmacked area next to the river.

Lots of people were out walking their dogs, roller-blading, or jogging.

What to do when you're in a park with people skating around you isn't in the highway code and didn't come up while I was learning to drive. I imagined it would tell one to drive slowly as there are children and people walking dogs around, so that's what I did.

The path ended and there was a barrier stopping pedestrians from going any further. There was a chain with a padlock on. I told the policeman I'd made a wrong turning and asked if he could let me out, he unchained the barrier and let me out.

## Back in Reality

Dad installed a letter board onto a laptop and brought it in to help me communicate. A computer solution seemed like a good idea because I'm a bit of a geek. I worked on computers; I had games installed on my PC at home; I had an Xbox 360; I had one of those little headsets with a microphone on it. I even had a gaming chair (is this painting a picture of a cool dude in your mind?).

A mouse was plugged in as I would find that easier to use than the built in touchpad. It was immediately clear that my right arm was behaving as it did when operating the fan. I was trying to reach for the mouse, but my arm was waving around. It took many detours, but eventually reached the mouse. I forgot to try and grab it and knocked the mouse off the table.

The mouse was picked up off the floor and placed back on the table.

I had another go, but my right arm was waving around again, making it trickier than this simple manoeuvre should have been. I eventually reached the mouse and now realised that my hand wasn't in the right position.

I straightened my fingers. It didn't hurt, but they felt stiff.

Moving my hand into a horizontal position was uncomfortable. It was like when you've slept on your hand forcing it into an unnatural position. I couldn't bring my hand all the way to horizontal; my wrist wasn't strong enough.

With my hand marginally better aligned, though still not in an ideal position, I knocked the mouse off the table. Again.

The mouse was picked up and placed back on the table.

I tried to hide my bubbling anger. I didn't stare at the mouse and think 'Right, just take your time. You might not be able to do this like you used to.' I just rushed to grab it again as though I was against the clock, doing exactly as I did before.

They say the definition of insanity is doing the same thing again and again and expecting different results.

My right shoulder began to hurt as though it was sprained. It felt as though it would squeak when it moved, that it was creaking. Some WD40 would have helped.

My right hand started to ache, as though enough blood wasn't getting into my hand. It felt like a Chinese burn.

I was trying to use the computer as I always had by not looking at the mouse and just looking at the computer screen. I thought I'd know where the mouse was and could sense how close to the edge of the table it was. I didn't take into account that I was working with double vision. The mouse wasn't where I thought it was.

Inevitably I pushed the mouse off the table with the right side of my palm like I was pushing it out of the way.

The mouse was picked up off the floor and placed back on the table.

My anger was probably quite noticeable now and it was obvious to me I wasn't going to be able to do it. I had no inclination to carry on other than to try to please people.

Both arms had been resting motionless in bed. Why was only my right arm behaving so erratically? I seemingly had full control over it, but it felt distant.

I couldn't share this with anybody at the time and once again knocked the mouse onto the floor.

It was picked up and I had another try.

I tried it more slowly, taking time to prepare my hand to grab the mouse. I hovered my hand over the mouse first and adjusted my fingers so the mouse would fit snugly in my hand. I moved my hand down and pushed the mouse onto the floor.

I grunted and sulked like a teenager. This was a soul-destroying defeat.

# Wall Pin

The computer solution had been a failure. Mum and Dad bought a cardboard letter chart and brought that in. My recollections of this are sketchy, so over to Dad again.

**The recovery graph seemed to be climbing steadily at this point, so Eva (Tom's Mum) and I brought in a large letter card with reasonable confidence of at last opening a communication channel. We showed it to Tom, who nodded his willingness to try it.**

**The results were disappointing. His hand wandered around the board without settling on any definite letter. He kept trying and control reappeared sufficiently to deliver his first message.**

**"Hdzg vjvt."**

**Either he'd learned an obscure eastern European language, or this wasn't working.**

**Over the ensuing days we tried again with similar results. Then it happened: the first coherent word.**

**"Remove"**

**We looked at each other. This was happening.**

**"Wall"**

**We looked at the wall, which looked challengingly solid. But Tom was still chatting.**

**"Pin."**

**He sank back into his pillows and closed his eyes, clearly exhausted by the conversation.**

**Eva looked at me. We didn't have much to say to each other.**

As Head of Rehab, Dr Soryal was overseeing my recovery at the Q.E. It fell to him to deliver difficult news to Mum, Adam and Laura.

He told them that there would almost certainly be permanent and severe disability. The control of my right arm was inaccurate, but relatively functional. However, my left arm and leg would be permanently inactive.

My mother pointed out that she'd seen me move both.

"Yes, but he's not moving them. Those limbs are perfectly healthy, but they're not receiving messages from the brain."

He explained that, as far as could be ascertained at the time, there was no cognitive damage, and that there most definitely would be quality of life in the future but, as Mum told me later, none of them could imagine how this could be true.

I remember Eva and Adam arriving home that evening. I'd been at some business meeting and had missed the daily visit. Tom's progress over the last week or so had been positive, so I was unprepared for the sorrow on their faces as they told me the news.

The next day, Dr Soryal invited us into his office. He apologised that he'd given such devastating news so clumsily the previous day. I should say here that this is one of the kindest and most empathetic men I've ever met. He was neither clumsy nor insensitive; it's a measure of the man that he cared so intensely that it might have been.

"Nothing is certain about recovery from a brain injury. I want you to understand the most likely prognosis, but you must continue to hope. Be ready for the worst, but pray for the miracle."

Keep those words in mind; you'll hear them again shortly.

After the failure of the letter board, Tom remained largely uncommunicative. One evening I tried to entertain him with my inexpert views on international rugby. I commented that England beat Australia by four points in 2003.

Tom's lips moved. I looked up at Eva.
I leaned closer to Tom. "Did you say something?"
"Three," he whispered.
That was all we heard from him for several months after, but it was a breathtaking milestone. Not only had he spoken, but he remembered events from before the operation.

My brother and his partner made several visits. Kaz is a yoga teacher and a remarkable healer. She suggested an exercise she called cross-crawl, in which the subject, lying on his or her back, moves their arms and legs in the same way a bear crawls. Tom couldn't do this by himself, so we each took a limb and began the movements, left arm down, right leg up, right arm down, left arm up and so on. Slowly he began to assist.

Around a week later, Dr Soryal was making his rounds when he saw Tom moving all four of his limbs without assistance. His surprise gave way to a delighted smile. He pointed at me.
"You've been praying for the miracle."

As my recovery continued, Dr Soryal suggested transfer to a specialist rehabilitation hospital. We were given the choice of two and chose the Haywood in Stoke-On-Trent as being the most convenient. Dr Soryal recommended it as the better clinical option too, and promised to enquire if a place was available.

A few days passed; the wait was like waiting for an envelope to fall through your letterbox telling you you've been accepted to your preferred University. Dr Soryal returned with the news we were hoping for. I was in.

## Stokeward Bound

An ambulance transferred me to the Haywood in Stoke-On-Trent. Mum, Dad and Laura went in Dad's car and I have a memory of them getting there a while before me.

I was transferred onto a gurney from my hospital bed and taken down on the lift and rolled through a warren of corridors. Dark blue signs adorned the walls. Fluorescent lights scrolled by above me. The ramp was already down on the ambulance, and the two paramedics pushed me into the ambulance, secured the bed and put a belt across my legs and chest, pinning me down – presumably in case I escaped.

One of the paramedics stayed in the back with me. As I was lying down, I could only see out of the top half of a window on my left and out of a skylight in the roof of the ambulance.

The journey seemed to take forever. I remember seeing the tops of buildings out of the window and I looked for the Parkour lads that had entertained me in hospital. They were closer this time, but still they were sprites from a 1980s computer game.

As we neared the hospital there was a large field running alongside the road. We took a right turn and turned onto a bumpy dirt track. We were thrown about as the ambulance's suspension tried to cope with the sudden off-roading. We came to an abrupt halt at the back entrance to the hospital.

The Haywood hospital was actually in a built-up area. We would have turned left into a side street and then right into the entrance for the rehab unit which is in its own car park. There's no trace of a dirt track.

It's possible I should have put some of this under Fragmented Memories.

# *Chapter 6 - The Haywood, Shunts and John Bonham*

### An Idiot Doing Idiotic Things

A friend of mine had told me she was selling her relatively new sofa. She and her husband had bought a corner sofa which suited their living room more. She described the sofa to me

"It's slightly longer than a three-seater. It's big enough for you to lie flat on without having to rest your head on the arm. It's cream and there's a small pouffe that goes with it."

She only wanted two hundred pounds.

"We'll take it!" I said impulsively. "I'll rent a van and we'll come and get it at the weekend."

I told my girlfriend who'd only relented to my impulsive desire to buy the house in the first place if I promised we could get kittens. I accepted the compromise happily because I wanted cats as well.

A house isn't a home without cats.

I hired a van and we drove over to collect the sofa. Fortunately, it was as described as I hadn't seen it up to this point. As I knew this person, I wanted to give the impression I was confident in this situation; an impression that might suffer if I got Laura to haggle with her. I handed over the cash and put the sofa into the van with the help of her husband.

I must give a child-like and immature vibe because the husband offered to back the van out of the drive as he didn't think I'd manage it.

I meant to say, "Nah you're alright mate, I've got this"

What came out was, "Yes please" as soon as he said "do you want me t-".

I chucked him the keys.

We got home and I realised the first problem: storage.

I hadn't got the house yet, and I'd never had to store anything because I lived with my parents and didn't own anything.

My parents had a long garage but there was no way a whole sofa could fit in among my Dad's years of accumulated stuff. My girlfriend's parents also had a long garage, but the back half of it was now a utility, so it wasn't very big any more.

Fortunately, Daniel needed a new sofa and agreed to take mine for the time being. With the van still legally mine for another few hours I made the short trip to his house. And discovered another problem: it wouldn't fit through the door. We unscrewed the feet and managed to squeeze it through.

Then I realised the third problem; the living room door is at a right angle to the front door. Directly behind the front door were incredibly steep stairs that you'd need crampons to climb.

I don't know how we managed it, but we got the sofa into the living room in one piece, although the wall was now the colour of the sofa and the sofa the colour of the wall.

It was then I realised the fourth problem. The living room was tiny. It would have looked crowded if it had been furnished with dolls' house furniture. Daniel was aware it was barely going to fit, but he had little choice as his younger brother is an idiot who buys things without knowing where to put them.

'Ah well,' I thought 'Got away with that one!'

After successfully palming that problem onto someone else, I returned the van.

It was our moving day a few months later and so I got a similar van and Adam came with me to pick up the sofa. Actually, I went with Adam as he did all the driving.

We got to Daniel's, packed it into the van and the three of us headed for my house.

Unsurprisingly, it wouldn't fit through my door either. We took the feet off and just about got it in.

And up came problem five. It was too big.

Considerable swearing and knuckle-smashing later, we shoehorned it against the only wall long enough to accommodate it.

And now the door to the hall and stairs wouldn't open.

I'm an idiot. You're welcome.

## Back in Reality

I was wheeled into the Haywood. We followed the corridor until it took a sharp left. The floor was dark green and slightly rough. The walls were white with no pictures. To the right was a slope down to the rehab unit. Straight ahead was the physiotherapy ward.

Reaching the rehab unit at the bottom of the slope you'd find the nurses' station to your right. The first of three wards was on the left and I saw a nurse through the glass. I thought she was sitting behind a screen as if she were a clerk at the Post Office. There was a strong aroma of lunch, so I guess it was around lunch time.

## Fragmented Memories

When I arrived, I was taken to a room with three other beds and I was to wait here to be checked in. In my memory Daniel was with me, but I now know that he wasn't. In fact few of my recollections match reality.

The nurse who checked me in may have been one whose name I later learned to be Jane, but my remembered room doesn't match any of those that made up the rehab unit.

## Another Fragmented Memory

Once checked in, I was put in a much bigger room that seemed to me like a school sports hall. Patients lay in beds around the perimeter of the room and then there were several rows of two beds in the middle of the room.

A female and a male nurse introduced themselves before they went upstairs to prepare my room.

Through the window of the sports hall I saw a footpath beside a road. Across the road were some houses.

A door, exactly like the front door of a house, lead outside. Patients and visitors would go outside to smoke a cigarette. It was opening and closing regularly as there seemed to be dozens of people around.

Directly in front of me were two interior doors, one of which led into a school gym where a netball game was being played. I have no idea what was behind the other door.

## Another Fragmented Memory

I could hear a radio blasting, playing the last interview Jeremy Beadle gave before he died on the 30$^{th}$ of January 2008. I think I was transferred to The Haywood in early February. I'm not sure how I heard that Jeremy Beadle had passed away, or why it stuck in my mind.

The radio was painfully loud. I tried desperately to get to it to turn it off, but I struggled to move. The side railings of the bed were raised and I tried to grab them to drag myself along, but I couldn't get a grip on the railings with my claw-like hands. Then Daniel suddenly appeared as if by magic and turned the radio down.

Dad's recollection of the day may be more reliable.

**This day is engraved on my memory. It was our first visit to the Haywood since Tom's arrival, and we'd been reassured by the warmth of the staff. As we entered the ward, we were hit by a barrage of sound. A TV, turned up to the point of distortion blattered inconsequential news. Tom wasn't immediately visible. We located him in a dark corner, right next to the screeching television. He was surrounded by walls of padded rails and lay at the bottom of a roofless cell, his face twisted in abject terror. Daniel muted the cacophony and Eva soothed Tom while I went in search of someone to rage at.**

**I found Sue, a senior nurse who was to become one of Tom's best friends at the unit. She quickly defused my rage by matching it with anger of her own. Before I'd completely explained, she stormed into the ward to set matters right. By now all was quiet, but Sue's reaction to the slip made it clear that there'd be no repetition.**

**Things can come adrift in the best-run establishment, so I should be clear that the Haywood and its staff were superb. Where things had gone wrong on this occasion was the issuing of the TV remote to an almost completely deaf patient in the bed next to Tom's.**

## Back in Reality

My family had noticed towards the end of my stay at the Q.E. that I was becoming increasingly unresponsive.

Even though I couldn't talk, I'd been giving the odd head nod or shake and other almost relevant gestures. My responses might not always have made sense, but I was at least trying to understand and follow conversation. It was becoming noticeable that these responses weren't as frequent.

This concerned them. On mentioning this to staff at the Q.E. in Birmingham, they were reassured that recovery can be an up and down process.

The decline continued at the Haywood. Within a few days I seemed to have checked out altogether. Then Dad and Daniel noticed swelling on the back of my neck - a lump the size of a golf ball, like a bulge in a bicycle tyre.

They called a nurse over to look. She was extremely concerned also, and sent me for an immediate MRI scan.

The brain naturally has gaps inside it, called sinuses. They allow the brain to adapt to slight pressure changes. In my case, they were almost closed, indicating high pressure inside the skull. This could be fatal and needed to be reduced urgently. Almost certainly I would have suffered severe pain, probably on a similar scale to that before the operation, but fortunately I have no memory of it.

I was rushed to North Staffs for an emergency procedure. Mr Price (coincidentally the neurosurgeon who was going to do the original operation on the NHS) installed a shunt. This is a plastic tube that sits inside the skull. It provides drainage of excess cerebrospinal fluid when something causes the brain cavity's natural pressure regulation to fail. Opinions differ on its use. Professor Cruickshank, who performed the original operation, preferred to avoid shunt installation where possible as they increase the risk of infection. The North

Staffs Neurosurgeon preferred the increased risk to the risk of excess pressure build-up.

Whoever was right, a shunt was now required, and time was of the essence. Hopefully with the addition of the shunt I would regain lost ground and continue my recovery. However, there was a real possibility that the pressure had caused further brain damage.

A thin tube is attached to the shunt which runs down my body as far as my pelvis. The cerebrospinal fluid is released here (where it is released to, I don't know).

This is my extremely limited understanding of my shunt anyway. I wasn't really 'present' at the time. To be honest if people ask what the shunt does, I just shrug my shoulders and say "dunno, I just know there's something in my head that means my brain doesn't explode."

Once it was in, I started to improve almost immediately.

On the left side of my head just above and behind my ear is the shunt. It's obvious running your hand over the location but it isn't noticeable to the naked eye because of my hair. It feels like there is a stick or a small matchbox car inside my skull.

After I'd recovered from having yet more surgery I returned to the Haywood. This would be my home for the next ten months.

## Fragmented Memories

I constantly had my mouth cleared by a small suction tool because I felt there was an irritation. I'd learned that Dad had continually excavated it while I was out of it at the Q.E. This had influenced my belief that I constantly needed my mouth clearing.

The suction tool is like the contraption you find at the dentist. The procedure was quite tricky, as Dad was being instructed by somebody who couldn't tell him where the irritation was, and he couldn't see anything. He usually pretended to remove this phantom irritation to appease me.

## Another Fragmented Memory

I was in a large rectangular room (large rooms seem to be a regular occurrence). My bed was on the left-hand side by the entrance. On the opposite side, about twenty meters away, were two beds side by side.

My vision was quite blurry and I couldn't make out what I was looking at, so my mind coloured in the rest of the picture. It wasn't staying within the lines though.

The two beds were separated by a curtain, and the bed on the left was being kept as a shrine to John Bonham, the Led Zeppelin drummer.

John Bonham died in 1980 by choking on his own vomit after a day of heavy drinking; he didn't go near a hospital.

I don't know why my brain thought about John Bonham. I'm not a fan of Led Zeppelin; I don't think I've even thought of John Bonham before. Even in my befuddled state, I wondered why a hospital in Stoke on Trent should set up a shrine to a drummer from Redditch who died in Windsor. It's one of many useless facts I know.

There's an insight here into how my brain was working at the time. I was lucid enough to know how Bonham died, and how illogical it would be for a shrine to be set up in this hospital so many years after his death.

But that's what I could see.

I was arguing with myself, telling myself it was nonsense, but then doubt started to creep in. I started to think it might be real. 'Well I can see it and my eyes can't be lying.' I reluctantly relented, still unconvinced by this vision but assured myself that if I could see it, it must be true.

John Bonham's bed was against the wall, but behind the bed was a panel that would shoot upwards as if somebody had pushed a button on the starship Enterprise. I noticed that the panel was open now. There was a cave inside, no wider than the door, but it seemed to be quite deep. There was a vase of flowers on a plinth in the middle.

Flowers?

My uncertainty as to the validity of what I was seeing returned.

'This can't be real'.

I had no qualms with the science fiction door and the cave behind the wall though.

## Another Fragmented Memory

I was in my bed again, unable to move and with the guard rails up. I was confused as Mum and Dad had been here, but now they were gone.

I was convinced I was going to be gassed.

I was sure I had been given a drug. That could be the only explanation for my inability to move. 'It's too much of a coincidence that Mum and Dad aren't here' I thought, 'I bet they're in on it'. Panic was setting in and I struggled but was unable to pull myself up by the guard rails.

'It's no good!' I thought, 'I'm doomed.' Without any further fuss I was instantly calm. I closed my eyes and tried to sleep.

## Back in Reality

I was awoken one night by a nurse from the night staff. She was preparing to administer medication through the tube that was attached to my stomach.[5] I was convinced she was one of the male patients, dressed in drag and impersonating the nurse, so I tried to fight her off.

She stopped me from slapping her away by restraining my weak and flailing arms. There wasn't any danger of hurting her as I didn't have any likelihood of connecting.

---

[5] It was a thin yellowy clear tube that was a millimetre and a half in circumference, and inserted through a small incision above my belly button. It is known as a feeding tube or PEG.

She easily overpowered me, calmed me down and put the medication into my feeding tube. I gave up as it was pointless trying to resist her. I just settled down and went to sleep. Rather than raise the alarm about somebody posing as a nurse roaming around, I had a kip.

## Fragmented Memories

I had some photographs on the wall above my bed. There were pictures of my friends, my niece and nephew, my cats Molly and Archie, and a publicity photograph of Jeremy Clarkson, Richard Hammond and James May from their journey to The North Pole for Top Gear. I explained to a sceptical nurse that my brother Daniel had gone out to the North Pole with my Dad and Uncle and taken the publicity photograph.

It's an interesting memory because this was some months before I regained the ability to speak.

# *Chapter 7 - Diary, Torture Devices and Washing & Dressing*

### An Idiot Doing Idiotic Things

It's 2001, and for my eighteenth birthday Daniel had bought tickets to see Sven Göran Eriksson's first game in charge of England at Villa Park.

England had played their final game at the old Wembley in the previous October – a dreary one-nil defeat to Germany. For the next seven years England would play their home matches at different grounds around the country.

I was beyond excited; I'd never been to an England match before and there was a lot of buzz around Sven's appointment. There was plenty of optimism that he could inject some life back into the England setup, which had become quite stale.

Villa Park was the perfect setting. It's always been one of my favourite grounds. It's fairly close to home and isn't massive, but still fairly big as it fits 40,000+.

As we emerged on the second tier of the Holte End, the pitch came into view. It was lit by floodlights and looked magical. It was as if somebody had laid a vast green carpet.

We took our seats and they gave us a brilliant view, I couldn't have wished for better.

We arrived about forty-five minutes before kick-off; my determination not to be late meant that we were far too early.

The stand filled as kick off approached. I was like a kid at Christmas, cheering wildly as the first players jogged onto the pitch.

I'd often wondered how chants get started at a match – they've got to start somewhere, so I decided to start one.

"COME ON ENGLAND, COME ON ENGLAND!"

Nobody joined in, and a lady in her early eighties, sitting in front of me with a blanket covering her legs, turned around and scowled at me.

I looked at Daniel and rolled my eyes. "Just my luck to be sitting behind the one person who doesn't like noise."

I turned my attention back to the pitch and noticed the players at whom I was chanting were, in fact, Spanish.

## Back in Reality

The staff kept a diary of my progress during my stay.

Many entries wouldn't make for very exciting reading. If you would like to know what physio I did on a certain day, or to read messages about nurses requesting an electric razor, just ask. Bit weird though.

```
27/02/08
Today Toms been on the tilt table to stretch his calf
muscles and stimulate his lower limbs he tolerated
this well for about ½ hr. We hoisted him into the
blue armchair, he sat in a very good position for 1½
hrs and he remained comfortable.
Claire G(physio)
```

The first thing to mention is this first torture, sorry 'physio' session, took place on the day of my twenty-fifth birthday.

"Congratulations, you're a quarter of a century old, now lie on this table and we'll hurt you for half an hour."

I joke of course… It was more like thirty-five minutes.

## Torture Devices

The physios collected me for my first session. As we neared the destination, I saw a mist-shrouded apparatus at the end of the room. As the mist faded I saw it.

The tilt table.

As we drew closer I could hear *Carmina Burana* getting louder and louder. The physios were cackling to themselves, surreptitiously high-fiving each other. I heard one of them say "another victim" while rubbing her hands together.

With the benefit of hindsight, I can see the tilt table was a massive success. I've had an awful lot of physio over the years and, even though nothing compares to the pain of the tilt table, my later progress wouldn't have been achievable if I hadn't been subjected to its torture.

I would likely have transferred to the tilt table using a slide board although I have no memory of this on this occasion. But as it's relevant to other moments during my stay, I'll explain it here.

The slide board is a shiny plank. One end of the board would be placed over the rear wheel of my wheelchair and the other end on the tilt table. I would then lift myself onto the board and slide a few inches down to the tilt table.

The tilt table is a medieval torture device that the NHS claims is an important tool. It's a slightly padded bed on which the patient lies, securely strapped by belts across the chest and legs.

My feet are against a rest at the bottom of the table. The cackling physio mutters to herself "I'm so happy right now" as she pushes a button and the table starts tilting until it's vertical and I'm in an upright position.

Before I tell you about my first time on the tilt table, let me explain some physical issues I now have.

When my brain stem was starved of oxygen, some of the nerve pathways were damaged. Among them were the wiring that allows parts of the body to tell the brain what position they're in. This is particularly important when they're at rest, because the brain can tell them how to relax. In my case, some of the messages were getting lost and some of my muscles were making their own minds up.

One result is that my pelvis is now tilted to the right – the space between my right hip bone and my ribcage is narrower than the width of a finger. That's not ideal, but my brain's not receiving any complaints, so it's taken as normal. As was soon to be revealed by the tilt table, it was anything but.

Anyway, back to the torture.

I absolutely hated the tilt table. Hate, **hate**, HAAAAAATE! The discomfort was awful.

The twist in my pelvis effectively lengthened my left leg while shortening the right. Once upright, my right foot didn't reach the footrest.

I'd been bed ridden since November 26th. That was four months of not supporting my own weight. Now I was being forced by these heathens to support my own weight.

I couldn't tell them that I was doing it on one leg - partly because I couldn't speak, but mainly because I didn't realise that the cause of my discomfort was having legs of unequal length.

Unknowingly I was putting most of my weight through my left leg and leaning over to the right so my right foot could reach the floor.

The physio told me I wasn't standing correctly, I was tilting to the right.

Again, I couldn't explain my problem. I wanted to say, "I thought I was straight. I won't be able to reach the floor your way."

Instead, I corrected my stand in the way I believed she was asking, by moving my torso to the left giving the appearance I was straight. Putting too much weight on my right leg created pain in my ribcage on that side.

I felt unsteady and unsafe, even though I was strapped in and couldn't go anywhere. I was grabbing mid-air with both hands to try and stay upright. This sudden movement of my arm hurt my right shoulder. My fingers felt as though the skin was stretching over my knuckles. I felt that my right Achilles was tearing because my leg wasn't long enough to reach the ground if I stood with a straight foot.

I sagged in the straps, but the physios seemed to be satisfied with my attempts. I hadn't indicated there was a problem; I'd just done what they'd asked. As far as I was concerned, I was standing.

I was frustrated. I'd never had to think about standing before, it was something that came as natural as breathing. It was a shock to me how difficult this was now, I wasn't mourning the loss of this ability, I wasn't upset that this obviously meant I wasn't going to be able to walk. I was just annoyed.

Annoyance was an emotion that would become quite familiar to me.

Not content with one form of torture, the physios decided to re-introduce me to an old friend…

Remember I told you about the dreaded blue chair at the Q.E. in Birmingham? Well, they had one at the Haywood too. And it was blue. It could at least have been a different colour so as not to trigger my PTSD when I saw it.

A hoist would be used to transfer me to the dreaded blue chair. It was like a miniature version of an industrial crane you might see on building sites. It was about six feet tall and could take considerable weight. It was on castors and two nurses had to be present to use it. An arm reached out from the top of the device and a sling hung down to hold the patient.

One of the nurses would move the arm down so that the sling could be placed under my bum. I'd be instructed to roll in a direction or lift a limb. I'd then be lifted into the air and rolled to my destination.

## Washing & Dressing

*29/02/08*

```
Written in retrospect. Physio on Thursday involved a
joint session with the Occupational Therapist to
perform washing + dressing. Thomas was supported in
sitting and managed to lift his head well and bring
the flannel to his face. Physio Charlotte spoke to
Thomas's brother Daniel to arrange for him to attend
a physio session on Friday.
```

Sister Landis

This is a good opportunity to tell you that I have Ataxia. It's a condition that can occur when parts of the brain or nervous system are damaged. It affects muscle coordination, causing tremors, speech difficulties, impaired vision and problems with precise movements.

The commencement of occupational therapy began to reveal how many of these symptoms affected me.

My first session began with an occupational therapist sitting beside me. I was seated on a physio bed next to a washing bowl, but couldn't stay in an upright position. I was swaying around as if drunk. The OT gripped my shoulders and held me close to her so that I had no room to sway.

My task was to pick up a flannel and wash my face and chest.

I picked up the flannel between the fingertips of my right hand but couldn't hold it without my hand shaking violently. The flannel felt like a squirming cat trying to free itself from my grip.

I dropped the flannel.

It was picked up, handed back to me and I reached for it with my left hand. I had no problem holding it this time and held it in a more natural way.

This was the side that Dr Soryal had predicted to be the most affected, but it appeared to behave as it should. I wasn't aware of his prognosis at the time, so I used my left arm without hesitation.

I had stood on my left leg on the torture device and my left arm was behaving itself. It seemed as though the left side was actually my *good* side.

Holding the flannel in my left hand felt different. I had more sensation; I could feel the roughness of the material. The right felt as though I was wearing a glove.

I transferred the flannel to my right hand, ensuring there was a large chunk of material between my fingers this time. This allowed me at least to maintain my grip.

I submerged the flannel and moved it towards my chest. My arm started veering right and left and my shoulder felt as though it was creaking like a rusty gate hinge.

The flannel reached my chest, but I was holding it for convenience rather than practicality, so I wiped my chest mostly with the back of my hand and a bit of the flannel.

This was a measure of success, but now my arm started to shake uncontrollably.

This is a classic symptom of Ataxia, although I didn't know that at the time.

This shaking is known as an intention tremor. It becomes obvious and exaggerated as the need for specific movement increases.

The OT took the flannel off me and showed me how I should be holding it.

My arm was still shaking, but I took the flannel, clutching it firmly. Immediately the cat squirm began again. I loosened my grip and my hand became calmer. It was still trembling, but I was able to hold on to the flannel.

I then started a habit I'm still trying to shake to this day. My whole body tenses as I try to stabilise my arm. I tense my right shoulder and I tense my right and left legs.

As my left foot was flat on the floor, I jammed it hard into the ground. This pushed me backwards, so I was leaning against the OT's arm, not even attempting to support myself. My right foot, which was reaching the floor by the tip of its toes, was now hovering.

I still do this today, when I try to write, pick up a glass, or even make myself heard in a noisy room.

```
29/02/08

Physio session with Daniel this a.m. Managed about
10 mins on the tilt table in a fairly upright
position. Feet were able to achieve a good position.
Tom less anxious today than last attempt on tilt
table. He responded well to instructions on placing
his feet.
                              Charlotte PT
```

I believe Charlotte is the physio I hit in the stomach with my right hand...

She left shortly afterwards. I'm sure this had nothing to do with her decision to leave... hopefully.

Maybe I should explain the circumstances.

I was quickly building a reputation as a bit of a problem patient. I still hadn't been completely aware of things at the Q.E.; I'd been mainly just lying in bed, staring at the ceiling, daydreaming about lads doing Parkour.

I'd managed to keep my anger hidden when I was exposed to the torture device that was the comfy blue chair.

At the Haywood I spent most of the early days in discomfort. Every day I was made to lie on a table that was flipped ninety degrees to the sound of my torturers high-fiving and boasting "He fell for it again!" I thought I hid my displeasure well, but their interpretation of what happened suggests otherwise.

I now had a very elaborate flinch reaction. If a part of my body touches something unintentionally, I react with an unpredictable lurch in any direction.

I knocked my elbow against something, triggering one of these elaborate reactions. My arm jerked away, striking Charlotte in the midriff.

I couldn't explain that this was accidental, so Daniel and Charlotte interpreted it as a 'lash out', reinforcing my declining reputation.

I also punched Daniel in the face…

I can't remember the circumstances. I suspect he was on the receiving end of my daily anger. Fortunately, my power and coordination weren't up to inflicting damage, and all I managed was more like when a baby puts a hand on your face and pushes it away. It didn't hurt, but I still received a telling off.

A nice way to thank him for visiting me every day!

# *Chapter 8 - Hand/leg Splints, Humiliation and Double Vision*

### An Idiot Doing Idiotic Things

It's 2006 and I've just bought a house.

A week after moving in, part of the soffit board fell onto the front garden. It was made of wood and had rotted away. While we waited for work to start, a squirrel spotted the hole and decided to accept my invitation and set up home in the attic.

After being woken by its scuffling on a few mornings, we decided something needed to be done. Feeling momentarily manly I told Laura I'd go up into the attic and see if it had caused any damage.

I leapt onto the banister and pulled myself up through the access hole. Feeling secretly proud that I was able to pull my own body weight, I sat with my feet dangling through the access hole while I looked around the attic.

"All good, I'm coming down".

But, I couldn't work out the mechanics of lowering myself and then dropping without breaking my arms.

"My arms don't bend that way; you'll have to get a chair"

Laura was doubled up laughing at my ridiculous predicament.

We hadn't got a chair, so I asked her to go round to my parents and borrow the step ladder.

"Really?" She questioned, while in tears of laughter. "Just jump!"

I insisted I couldn't.

So with me stranded while a savage squirrel was on the loose, she drove thirty seconds up the road to my parents' house to pick up the ladder.

She was helpless with laughter as she explained the situation to my Mum. My sympathetic mother was now also doubled up and agreed to loan the ladder, but only if I brought it back in person.

Fortunately, when my girlfriend got home I wasn't writhing around on the floor with two broken arms and a savaged and bloody face from escaping the squirrel's vicious attack.

I climbed down and was told my Mum insisted on my personal return of the ladder.

After my near-death experience I wasn't in the mood to be laughed at. I propped the ladder against the house, knocked the door and ran off.

## Back in Reality

```
4/3/08
I have made Tom a new hand splint on both hands. We
need to build up his tolerance to them over the next
few days. There is a splint chart in his blue folder
so that we can record how long Tom is wearing them
for in one go. I am aiming for 2 hours this evening,
then 3 hours tomorrow and 4 hours on 6/3
                                            Thanks Alice
```

I had been at the Haywood for about a month now and I had been steadily improving. Gone were the days of falling asleep during visiting hours.

Most days I adhered to a routine which ended with bedtime, and started when the day on the ward began. There were some days when I would have a nap in the afternoon but that never meant I couldn't sleep at night.

Alice had been wanting to tackle the issue of my hands as they wouldn't remain in a normal resting position. They were still bent sharply down at the wrist and my fingers were bent like claws. I could straighten them, but as soon as I relaxed, they'd bend again.

Sorry, that's rude of me. Let me introduce you to Alice.

Alice was the head occupational therapy and oversaw my case from the OT side of things.
    I had a lot of fun with Alice; she liked a laugh and a joke. She was more like a friend.
    I had monthly goal planning meetings and she was always in attendance. She would come and see me just to check how I was getting on. She got on well with my family too, fitting in seamlessly with their silliness.

However, my opinion of Alice would be completely different if it was based solely on her decision to make me wear hand splints.

I had already known Alice for about a month. She had obviously used that time to gain my trust…
    I'm sure Alice was trying not to cackle as she informed me of the plan. She was rubbing her hands together excitedly as she told me I would wear them every night.
    She made a point of saying, "I didn't have any blue splints, but don't worry, these will be just as… *effective*".

Wearing the splints in bed would force my fingers, wrist and hand to stay straight, meaning eventually my wrist would rest in a natural position. A nurse would put these splints on my hands before I went to bed and would take them off me whilst I was sleeping.

The hand splints fitted along the underside of my arms, from the forearm to the fingers. They were beige and were secured by three extremely efficient horizontal Velcro strips that were all located just above the wrist. Once the straps pressed against the Velcro they were incredibly difficult to get off. Another horizontal strap secured the fingers, forcing them into a natural position.

That was the theory anyway, the reality of it was quite different.

I never wore them for the required time. It was difficult to get to sleep because my hands were aching so much.

The first night they were put on me I was reminded by the nurse "I'll take these off after two hours - while you're asleep."

She walked away and I wanted to shout, "GET THEM OFF!" But I couldn't and she continued to walk away.

They immediately caused discomfort. I realised this wasn't going to be straightforward, but all I had to do was fall asleep. How hard could that be?

I shut my eyes and waited for slumber to take me. I wasn't remotely tired though; my fingers felt as though they were being bent backwards.

A few minutes passed, 'Just grin and bear it'. I told myself. This went on for about ten minutes.

I just wanted to sleep, so I decided to take them off. My right arm started to shake, seemingly nervous about the escape attempt.

I hadn't the fine control in my right hand. My fingers were secured and I couldn't see the straps without the lights on.

I tried to take off the right-hand splint first because my left hand was more accurate. I picked at the corner of the Velcro to loosen enough of the strap so that I could pull it. I found what felt like a strap, but I couldn't free it from the Velcro. I think it had been stuck with super glue.

I contemplated using the call-nurse remote, but I imagined how the conversation would go. I would gesticulate wildly, my disapproval evident, but without speech the nurse would just say, "They need to be kept on I'm afraid" and walk back to the nurses' station unaware of the expletives I was thinking.

I lay in the dark for what felt like ages, picking away.

I turned up enough of the strap to grab it and finally managed to free it; now I just had to free the others.

I freed my right hand which should have meant that the next splint would be easier.

My right arm was shaking. Fortunately, I now knew how the straps were laid out. The reduced feeling in my right hand meant that I couldn't tell from touch alone.

I picked away at the strap until there was enough to grab. My hand waved around as I tried to grip it, but there was only a small corner free, and I couldn't get enough purchase. I needed to excavate a bit more.

I freed enough but my hand kept slipping off and hitting the bars at the side of the bed. I was going to wake people up.

I finally managed it, tossed the splints to the foot of the bed and thought about how close I came to... well, a few hours of slight discomfort.

I wonder who'll play me in the movie...

Each morning Alice would ask the nurses how long I had worn them and the answer was never the required time.

```
5.3.08
I've reviewed Tom's swallow again today and re-
introduced some trials of pudding/thick fluids or
equivalent. If you think there is something else
please let the nursing staff know. The other area we
are going to work on is the movement of his lips +
tongue in order to encourage more activity. This will
be beneficial for speech + swallowing. I will see Tom
again next week.
          Lois Dale SLT (speech and language therapy)
```

I was able to start taking sips of water, though I wasn't trusted to pour it myself. A jug was left by my bed and I would buzz for a nurse when I wanted some.

Mum brought in some cordial, and the nurse would dilute it and put in a teaspoon of thickener. This was added to drinks to give them some volume so that I could swallow them without choking.

The powder would start reacting as soon as it touched the water and the nurse would then stir it until it was as thick as wallpaper paste. She knew it was ready for me to drink when the spoon would stand upright on its own. It had the consistency of treacle, and had small bits of something that looked like grains of sugar. It was flavourless so as not to alter the taste of the drink, but the consistency was altered so much I could chew it.

I hadn't had any solid food since my operation. I was hydrated by a drip and sustained via the feeding tube connected to my stomach.

When the other patients went to the dining hall, I would be spoon-fed yoghurt by a nurse. Each spoonful consisted of a small coating of yoghurt, as swallowing more would make me cough.

When one breathes in, air goes down the larynx towards the lungs. Food follows the same route until it reaches the larynx. A flap of skin called the epiglottis moves to block the entrance so that food particles and fluid don't get into the lungs.

I have dysphagia (difficulty swallowing) meaning mine doesn't always work properly, food and fluid sometimes follow the same route to the lungs which makes me cough.

The first few times I swallowed the yoghurt I coughed, as if I was trying my first cigarette.

"Slow down. Keep the yoghurt in your mouth for a few seconds, and then swallow it," instructed the nurse; advice that was quite useful because as usual I was rushing it.

I did as she suggested, giving my epiglottis time to get into position,[6] and almost immediately the nurse was able to put more yoghurt onto the spoon.

Quite early in my stay at the Haywood I may have had Botox injections in my wrist and shin. This could be a fragmented memory as I don't have a clear recollection and several things don't add up.

In fact...

## Fragmented Memories

I have to assume that it was the doctor who prescribed the Botox (if in fact anyone did) – it certainly wouldn't have been my suggestion, even if I could talk.

I was told that the doctor was retiring very soon and was "kind of a big deal" as he was at the very top of his profession. He had an air of importance about him, so if he did suggest it, then I didn't want to hold him up.

I don't know if Botox is administered by a single injection or several. Despite my movie-star looks, you'll be surprised to know I've never had Botox. I can vaguely remember a quick injection in my shin.

Could a Botox injection help me? As far as I know it's not known as a painkiller – and I don't think I was in pain anyway. It's usually used for getting rid of the lines on Gordon Ramsay's forehead.

---

[6] I should be clear this is my own explanation. As you're discovering, I think I'm a medical genius, but you *know* I'm an idiot.

As I don't know the intention, I can't confirm if it worked or not. My shin does look about ten years younger than the right though, so swings and roundabouts.

## Humiliation

```
6.3.08

Tom only managed two teaspoons of thickened fluids.
But when hoisted back onto the bed used a bottle
                                                    Sue
```

I wasn't able to visit the little boy's room yet, so I used a disposable cardboard container.

Unfortunately, the body uses two methods to get rid of waste and I was in a right panic about method number two.

I was trying to think of ways I could do this myself and I couldn't. I was adamant I wasn't going to crap in a box though.

My inner thoughts reminded me that I didn't control the situation and if the nurses wanted me to crap in a box, well, I'll have to crap in a box.

I held off for as long as possible but realised there was only one outcome here, and the sooner I get it over and done with, the sooner my humiliation is over'.

I called a nurse and apologetically signalled I needed to go to the loo.

I was imagining she was going to be horrified and shout out "CAN SOMEBODY GET A BEDPAN? TOM SHAW FROM THE SECOND WARD NEEDS A CRAP!"

Her response was immediate. Without missing a beat the nurse replied "OK" like I'd just asked for a cup of tea. The nurse went to the stockroom to get a bedpan and asked another nurse to get the hoist.

The blood drained from my face.

I thought there would be some discretion, but everybody on the ward was going to know what I was about to do. I assumed everybody would be watching as there is very little else happening on a hospital ward.

My previous reluctance to crap in a box was quickly forgotten as I realised I was going to be hoisted up prior to defecating into a box, like a cat using a litter tray.

A second nurse pushed the hoist over and drew the curtains. Something about the sling was unfamiliar. I couldn't see what was different, but something had changed.

With the brakes on I leant forward and the sling was placed between my back and the backrest of the wheelchair. A few seconds later I found myself suspended bottomless in a sitting position, with my backside poking through a strategically placed aperture. The box was slid into place.

It was incredibly embarrassing, but the embarrassment didn't end there…

I hadn't thought about what happens afterwards. I'm half-naked, hanging in mid-air, dangling over a cardboard box. I haven't enough control over my right arm to trust it with the next task. I've got to use the call button to signal I'm ready to have my arse wiped.

The indignity of this was awful, I was too embarrassed to look her in the eye and I'm fairly sure I apologised to the nurse. It wasn't an issue for her; she lowered me back to the bed while chatting as normal with me and her colleague.

It's amazing how quickly I got used to this. I was in the Haywood for ten months and this was a regular occurrence, but it's just part of the job as far as nurses are concerned.

The nurses were incredible. They were required to undertake all manner of similar tasks and always did it with a smile on their face and would laugh and joke with all of us. I never once saw them grumpy from the pressure we all know they are under. I could not have got through this without their kindness and generosity. They're incredible people and I'm sure they take great satisfaction from helping people like me who are completely helpless and not making us feel embarrassed. I can't thank them enough. The shame and embarrassment of this day after day for the entirety of my stay would have been unbearable, but they made it feel completely normal.

```
10.3.08 - speech + lang

I have seen Tom this morning and practised some lip
+ tongue exercises. Tom did well with the exercises
+ it would be really beneficial if you could practise
them with Tom aswell. I have left a sheet explaining
the exercises. 5 to 10 mins at a time would be great.

                        Thanks, Aimee (SLT assistant)
```

Aimee was the speech and language therapy assistant to Lois. She did most of my NHS-funded therapy as Lois went on maternity leave after a few months of my stay.

I would have a session with her twice a week. What could be done was quite limited at first because I couldn't talk. I'd imagine it was like trying to teach someone who's allergic to water to swim.

We would work on lip and tongue positioning as these would be important when I started talking again. It was never discussed *if* I would speak again. I always got the impression it was *when*.

Aimee provided exercise sheets that showed cartoon pictures of mouths and tongues in different positions. They illustrated where the tongue should be to make certain sounds like "oo" and "ee".

For all of the vowels, the tongue hovers in the middle of the mouth, playing little part in the sound. The position of the lips and slight changes to mouth shape decide whether you say "ah", "ay", "ee" and so on.

Consonants bring the tongue, throat and lips into play, some of the time with the aid of the vocal cords. Put your lips together and gently blow them apart and you're making a "P" sound. Let your vocal cords hum slightly and it's "B". But if you let some air escape, it sounds like "F" or "V".

You think you know all this, but you've probably never thought about it. You might not realise how precise those movements are. I had to learn all this again – and I couldn't even get my hands to land within a foot of where I was aiming.

Aimee tasked me with exercising for ten minutes each day. The exercises reproducing the mouth shapes on the sheets. I didn't show much enthusiasm for this after the first few practices. At first it was something new, so I spent the required ten minutes silently making faces at a piece of paper.

I've always been somebody that gives up if I'm not seeing immediate results. It wasn't completely clear how these grimaces could lead to actual speech, and their appeal quickly waned.

## Double Vision

Until my voice returned, we made another try at using a letterboard. My arm still waved around and would often begin to shake when used. It could take several seconds to select a letter, and sometimes the wrong one. For reasons I can't explain now, I'd continue spelling out a message even after the meaning had been guessed:

"Do you want a drink?"

My hand would wander around the board and eventually land near "Y"

"So that's a yes."

"Hang on, he's still spelling…"

"E"

"We've got it, yes, you want a drink."

"S"

"Okay, we understand."

"P"

"You don't need to say 'please'!"

…and so on.

My family put this down to brain injury. Idiocy may also have been a factor.

The communication channels were now open, and it's around this time I first told my parents that I thought I had double vision.

I overheard someone explaining their difficulty to the doctor, who gave the temporary solution of sticking tape over one of the lenses of their glasses.

'Hang on,' I thought. 'Maybe that's why I see two of everything.' Up until this point, I hadn't questioned why I had difficulty seeing properly. I didn't even know I was having difficulty.

The letter board allowed me to share my new understanding.

'G'
"Gee" would come the reply
'L'

'El' they would chorus

'A' while pointing at my eyes

"Glasses" they would answer.

I pointed at S

"Glasses" they would chorus.

I pointed again at the S.

"*GLASSES!*" they would raise their voices.

"*GLASSES!* Do you want your glasses?"

I aimed for E and landed on D.

"D? You mean E. You're spelling out *GLASSES!*"

They clearly knew what the answer was, but nothing could stop me. I would point to the final S

"S? no idea, spell it again." They'd say sarcastically.

I laugh silently, shrug my shoulders and point to G again.

"NO!" they would say ripping the letter board from my grasp.

I'm not sure how the rest of this conversation went but I obviously got my point across as there are pictures of me wearing my glasses with tape over one lens.

# *Chapter 9 - Connect 4, Stress, I've Got A Drink Problem and Look This Way*

### An Idiot Doing Idiotic Things

Shortly after I passed my driving test some friends and I were going to go down to London to watch Chelsea vs Blackburn Rovers.

I insisted on driving, so the four of us piled into my car and we started the trip down. I had got the directions off the Internet and as I was driving, somebody else was navigating so there was a good chance we would get there incident-free.

Wrong! Somebody else was navigating, but I was still driving, and, well, I'm an idiot…

Signs were appearing saying that the junction on the M6 we needed to take to switch onto a different motorway was closed.

I hadn't taken heed of these signs. When I took notice of the 'road closing' sign, cones were appearing in my lane and the way ahead was getting narrower and narrower until there was no lane left. I panicked and took the only option available to me.

'This exit is next to the one I was going to take,' I thought. 'It's got to go close to where I want to go.'

As we drove a little bit further, we were picking up signs to places that weren't in the directions we had, so one of my friends phoned his Dad, who worked for the AA.

"You're heading for Wales," his Dad informed us with noticeable bemusement in his voice.

He gave us directions to get back on track and we were soon heading the right way again, although we were now running considerably late, and I had to make up the time without going over the speed limit.

Amazingly we almost did it. No speed limits were broken (ok, this is a lie), but when we got into London it was extremely confusing. I think my brake pedal was attached to other people's horns as they sounded every time I braked to switch lanes.

There were looks of befuddlement as I stopped in the middle of a pedestrian crossing; I'd seen the amber light ahead and thought 'I can stop before the line' and slammed the brakes on. The bangs on the window from the pedestrians having to walk around my car told me I was wrong. I should have wound down the window and said "I'm Tom Shaw and I'm an idiot" but I don't think these people would have seen the funny side.

I saw an empty parking space, and in London that's as rare as rocking horse excrement. I decided we would park here and do the remaining mile on foot.

I parked and the four of us sprinted to Stamford Bridge. It was 14:55 and I re-assured everyone not to worry, I'm sure nothing will happen in the first few minutes.

We were next to the stadium, when the crowd erupted. Andy Cole scored...

## Back in Reality

```
Physio 10.3.08 10:00am

Really good session today

1 ½ hours in tilt table, Tom was relaxed, feet in a
good position

Reaching for objects - we need to encourage Tom to
reach with right arm/hand

20 mins in electric standing frame(OSF) - Tom relaxed
throughout & joining in the stand- Very well done

                                            Michelle
```

**Am I reading that right? One and a half hours on the tilt table, is it any wonder I had angry outbursts? It's just as**

well I couldn't speak because at least that meant I only said the profanities to myself.

While strapped to the tilt table, a physio would hold a plastic miniature cone in different positions - high, low, near, far, left and right. I was only allowed to reach for the cone with my right hand.

I would mostly do this exercise with a student nurse called Lydia, who was there on a work placement. She seemed to pick up the old torture regime very well.

After my first attempt I realised I couldn't reach very far. My shoulder felt sprained, creaking like an old gate hinge. The pain was stopping me from reaching very far. Lydia was aspiring to a career based on torture, so she encouraged me to push past the pain.

"Do you know what you should do?" She would say while covering her mouth with her hand. "Push past the pain."

The word 'pain' would be said at a higher register as she tried to stifle laughter.[7]

I tried to push past the pain, but found myself just leaning forwards as far as I could, straining against the straps. I was able to reach slightly further, but it didn't make much difference to the flexibility of my arm.

It was far easier when Lydia held the cone high on my right. I would still need to stretch, but the cone was virtually straight in front. Lydia knew I found this easier and would hold the cone on my left side. I could barely

---

[7] This almost certainly isn't true.

scratch an itch on the left side of my body, so this would be a stretch (pun intended).

I couldn't reach it. I tried my trick of leaning against the straps, and managed to brush it with the tip of my finger. My shoulder felt as though I'd torn a muscle, and the stretching left me out of breath.

The pain in my shoulder would sometimes still be there the next day. It seemed to take a completely random time to recover.

Some days it wouldn't recover until I went to sleep, it would even be uncomfortable to lie down. I'd lie on my back with my arms resting on the mattress, but this still put stress on my shoulder.

Lydia and I played *Connect 4* while I was standing on the tilt table. As you probably know, *Connect 4* pieces are a larger version of a two-pound coin. The outside is corrugated so that they're easy to pick up. For most people.

The pieces were lying flat in the lid of the box and I couldn't pick them up.

She held the board between us and I reached for a piece with my left hand, picking it up with ease.

"Ah, ah, ah" she said, metaphorically hitting me across the knuckles with a ruler. "With your right hand."

I reached to pick it up but couldn't lift the piece. I'd just push it around, constantly lining up my fingers to pick it up and nudging it away.

The only way I could grab it was to nudge it to the side of the box, push it against the side so it would raise up and give me more surface to grab.

I could then drop it into the slot... maybe.

I had no depth possession. I was wearing my glasses with the right lens covered, so I was only seeing a single image, but that meant the slot was further away than I thought.

The piece ended up on the floor a lot, until I learnt the hole was slightly further away than my eyes were telling me.

Even with these difficulties, I would beat her every time.

It's like she was letting me win...

This was the last time I used the tilt table. I'm not sure if it was because of my progress, or the physios wanted to try out new torture devices. I did see it in the distance sometimes and knew it was nearby when I could hear *Carmina Burana* playing in the distance.

The physio mentioned the standing frame (OSF) in the diary extract above. OSF stands for Oswestry Standing Frame. It's an ancient-looking thing, like something from the 1920s, but it's a clever bit of kit. It has bannisters either side for the patient to hold onto, and straps to keep them in position.

This one was deep enough to accommodate the front part of my wheelchair, and had its own wooden floor. At the front of it, at around waist height, was a desk. Underneath this was a belt running horizontally across the frame, against which the patient's toes would rest. Belts, covered in yellow nylon fur, were provided to support the knees and back.

As with the tilt table, it became clear that I was leaning to the right and putting all my weight on one leg. The physios gave me instructions to evenly distribute my weight. They physically moved my pelvis and torso into the correct position to show me where straight was.

This felt completely wrong, as if I was standing in an unnatural position. It felt natural the way I was originally standing; now I felt that I was leaning towards the left. My right side felt stretched. I couldn't explain this or ask questions, so I just went along as always.

Once I was standing straight. I did the same reaching exercises as with the tilt table and then finished off with a game of *Connect 4*.

I won again.

Lydia wasn't around this time. I think I was just amazingly good.

## Stress

```
Sunday 16th
Good morning. Tom watched some of DVD. Was keen to
sit up look around ward: We practiced looks to the
left as opposed to always the right.
```

I was able to avoid my communication issues by not being around people and watching films instead. I would put my headphones on which was the equivalent of putting a do not disturb sign around my neck.

I was fooling myself into believing I was fairly happy. I could just lie around watching DVDs, something I'd have liked to do before coming into hospital. However, I couldn't eat apart from yoghurt fed to me by nurses. I could only have drinks mixed with wallpaper paste, prepared by nurses. I'd be washed and have my arse wiped by nurses. I wasn't lifting a finger.

I was basically like Henry VIII, and nobody's got a bad word to say about him.

I couldn't imagine the days being bearable without films to distract me. What would I do? Have a nurse wheel me around so I can socialise and then expect people to wait patiently and guess what I'm spelling on the letter board?

Watching films exposed my concentration issues. Any word mentioned could send me down a rabbit hole of imagination. A character might say "shuttlecock" and that would start me thinking of when I was sitting my GCSEs in the sports hall and looked up to see a shuttlecock in the roof. Speaking of looking, I really should watch *Look Who's Talking* again. Wasn't the guy who played John Travolta's grandfather also the guy who played Tessio in *The Godfather*?'

My attention would eventually return to the screen, and I'd realise I hadn't a clue what was going on and would have to rewind.

Rewinding meant doing battle with the touchscreen, as the DVD player didn't have a remote control. I had to touch the screen so the progress bar would appear and then drag it back. I couldn't predict how far back I needed to go, so more often than not, I would rewind it further than needed. Then I'd wait to reach the right section, but I'd daydream, disappear down another rabbit hole, and not follow the film again.

When my attention returned to the film, Denzel Washington might be wearing some weird helmet contraption on his head that covers one of his eyes. And why is he driving a pickup truck?

Rewinding meant doing battle with the touch screen again.

I tried watching with the subtitles on, to force me to concentrate on reading what was on the screen and keep my focus on what was happening.

That was the theory, but I'd find myself drifting off just as often. I'd be close to tears, frustrated as I saw the clock winding towards the interruption of visiting hours or a physio session.

People would turn up for visiting and I would ask if they minded if I just finished this film. If I wasn't able to finish it, I couldn't concentrate on what they were saying. The film now felt like a job, a deadline I had to meet before I went to sleep.

I'd focus back on my visitors and wonder what they were talking about, but there was no rewind for this.

I'd go to bed feeling stressed and wake up hoping the nurses gave me my bed bath straight away so I had more time to finish yesterday's film before starting another.

## I've Got A Drink Problem

```
Tuesday 18th (pm)

Physio/OT

Worked on sitting on plinth. Also worked on good
patterns of movement in reaching with left arm to
grasp beaker and take to Tom's mouth. Stood a couple
of times, but session lasted for 1 hour and Tom was
tired! Put Tom back in bed, but Tom agitated and
managed to communicate that he wanted to sit in his
wheelchair! So Tom hoisted into wheelchair at 4.10pm.
                                                Alice
```

I'd had a few incidents when a drink was poured for me. Without thinking I reached for it with my right hand, resulting in the beaker being knocked over, or my hand shaking while holding the beaker.

There were many spillages. Fortunately, the nurses were on hand and there was so much thickener in the drink, the fluid was almost solid.

I needed to get into the habit of only using my left hand to pick up a beaker, but it felt unnatural.

I fired the Alice Signal into the sky and she answered the call.

The incidents I'd had before when using my right hand were still going to exist even if I was using my left hand. Because of my lack of depth perception, I thought the beaker was in a different location. I would close my fingers, expecting to wrap my hand around the cup, but push it further away or - in some cases - off the table.

I quickly learnt to allow for this but in this practice session the beaker didn't have much liquid in it; there was no spillage when I knocked the beaker or partially grabbed it.

It felt as though I was learning a dance routine, just learning the order to do things in, like a strictly choreographed routine.

I was reluctant to do this on my own at first. I was asking the nurses to fill my beaker three quarters of the way to avoid spillage. They saw through my tactic though, and encouraged me to use my left hand.

This felt somewhat of a risk and I had Alice in my head running through the choreography to help. I was nervously judging when I should close my fingers and grab the beaker, hoping that my eyes hadn't deceived me.

## Look This Way

```
11.3.08 Physio pm
Sitting work on plinth.
Reaching with L + R hands reaching for objects.
-> Work on looking to L with eyes + neck
-> Need to work on sitting to Tom's L and get him to
look that way. Good calm session. Tom said he enjoyed
it when asked - nodding.

                                          Lizzie Physio
```

I liked Lizzie, She was good fun. I even asked my parents to buy a green teapot for her as a leaving present when she left a few months into my stay.

I clearly was brain damaged, conveniently forgetting that she had gleefully taken part in my torture.

I should have got her a blue teapot.

While I was in the ICU, I'd lain on my back with my head turned to the right at a ninety-degree angle. I now couldn't turn my head to the left.

I could turn it to the centre, and then it felt as though there was a sheet of taut cellophane resisting me.

I was assured that the pain of trying would lessen the more I did it. Lizzie didn't appear to be cackling or rubbing her hands together with glee as she said it, so I tried it.

# *Chapter 10 – Bobath, The Speech Therapy Journey Begins and Temper, Temper*

Weds 19|03|08

Hello! Alice said she had mentioned Tom taking part in our Bobath course. I've left the consent form which needs to be signed if you are happy for Tom to take part. The letter explains what the course is about & the dates we will require Tom. Could you make sure Tom has plenty of shorts available to wear for the course please.

Poppy

The Bobath course was run by Lynne Fletcher. She runs a clinic called the Manchester Neurotherapy Centre (MNC), with her co-founder Linzi Meadows. Lynne teaches the Bobath technique nationally and internationally, having learned the concept from its founders. She became an Advanced Bobath tutor in 1993.

The physios at the Haywood spoke of Lynne with great respect and admiration, as I would imagine most physios in the country do. She travels around the country hosting sessions like this to teach some of the Bobath methods.

The head physio asked me if I wanted to take part as a model.

'Well obviously!' I thought. 'I'm the David Gandy of the rehab unit, I'm offended it took you so long to ask.'

It's more likely she wasn't asking me as eye candy though, she was thinking more along the lines of a mannequin that could be shaped into certain poses. I provided some unique challenges that Lynne could use to teach.

So, I agonised over this decision for days and managed to move some things around in my hectic diary. I tried to negotiate a fee, but it was clear I'd misunderstood their use of the word 'model'.

I got to the class and saw there were a number of other patients here, chosen I presume, because of their varying neurological problems.

A few of the hospital physios were in this class as well to offer some extra pairs of hands and to watch Lynne at work.

The majority of the session seemed to concentrate on me only. I don't know if there were other classes using other patients as models, but this one mainly focussed on my walking and posture. I was wearing shorts so the physios could see exactly what my legs were doing.

Up to this point, my walking sessions had involved three physios. Two would take my arms across their shoulders to support my weight; one would follow, guiding my hips. My main task consisted of hanging limply between them while walking happened.

Lynne, spent a few minutes examining my sitting position before taking hold of my hands and, gently but firmly, pulling me into a standing position.

Audible gasps came from the physios, but another miracle was to come. She stepped to my side and placed an arm around my waist. She encouraged me to take a step forward. I put my weight onto my left leg and swung my right leg forward. I slightly bent my left leg so that my right foot could reach the floor, and transferred my weight onto my right leg. The knee felt weak; I thought it would buckle. I leaned to the right, releasing my left leg. I thought this was an effective workaround, but now I was leaning, which Lynne didn't like.

"Stop leaning on me. Support your own weight."

I tried to keep my torso centred and put my weight through my fragile knee. My foot couldn't reach the floor, I had to reach it with the ball of my foot.

Lynne returned me to my seat and examined my hip and pelvis. She helped me to the floor where I lay on my back and endured a rather painful sports massage while Lynne explained to the physios what she was doing.

We had limited time and I'm not going to pretend I understand what Lynne did. It seemed similar to Mr Miyagi rubbing his hands together so that Danny LaRusso could compete at the end of *Karate Kid*.

I was helped to my feet and took a few steps. My walking didn't look very different, but Lynne's manipulation had made a difference to my ability to transfer weight onto my right leg. I wasn't having to lean; my knee still didn't feel as though it could take my weight, but it was clear to me now that I'd been using it as little as possible because of its inability to reach the floor.

```
8.4.08 Physio - Bobath

Tom had a really good session this morning with the
instructors. They worked on stretching out his right
hip from lying on the floor making it less stiff. Tom
was encouraged to keep his head relaxed in the middle
to enable him to strengthen his abdominal muscles and
leg muscle control. Tom used this activity to be
guided into standing from the floor with the physios.
This session was repeated in the afternoon with
smaller groups. Tom seemed to enjoy the session and
concentrated well.
                                                 Claire H
```

I indicated I wanted to get some exercise. I didn't think it would be possible because of my inability to stand unsupervised or stay upright.

I was taken up to the physiotherapy department to use the exercise bike, a brilliant piece of equipment called a Medimotion that I've encountered a number of times over the years.

It's a static exercise bike that doesn't have the frame of a bicycle, designed for use from a wheelchair. It has handlebars in front of a large colour display that measures the usual things like distance and calories burnt. Below it are the pedals, either side of the exercise wheel, which is covered by smooth grey plastic. Attached to each pedal is a large black foot-shell with two pieces of Velcro to secure one's foot.

I was set up on the bike and left to do some exercise. I started cycling very fast, and was eager to show everybody how physically fit I was. I imagined a crowd of people standing around me clapping and chanting "TOM! TOM!"

This wasn't the case. Fortunately, nobody witnessed me gasping for air with my arms draped over the handlebars.

I slowed down to the point of almost stopping, and a message popped up, "Motor is taking over". My legs continued moving but I wasn't making any effort.

While I was letting the machine do the work for me, I watched the readout slowly cycling through all of the displays - distance covered, speed, calories etc. A screen entitled 'symmetry training' showed a small bar graph with two bars, half filled. It showed the effort each leg is putting into the exercise.

I was fascinated by it. I was no longer interested in regaining fitness, I wanted to maintain this symmetry. A physio locked the display for me, and I started pedalling. Immediately the left bar filled to around eighty percent. The bars weren't symmetrical any more, and that frustrated me.

For the duration of my exercise, I tried to get this readout back to reading fifty percent on both sides. I couldn't do it. I could get close by slowing down, which was completely missing my original intention of exercise, but my attention was now fixed on getting these readings even.

I noticed just how thin my right leg was. I had always been wearing a gown or pyjama bottoms up to this point and I hadn't seen my legs.

I wondered why though.

Both of my legs were attached to the same body and were both bedridden for the same amount of time. Why had one leg withered more than the other?

I understood that my left leg had been doing most of the work when I was standing in physio, but surely not enough to make such a noticeable difference?

## The Speech Therapy Journey Begins

```
12.3.08 speech therapy
Please ask Barbara to contact me on xxxxx xxxxxx when
she has completed her initial assessment. I work
Tues, Weds + Fri so if I'm not available, please
leave a contact no so I can return the call.

                                     Regards Lois Dale
```

I first met Barbara Molteno in March. She came to the hospital and met Dad and me.

I can't remember the reason for meeting her, we certainly weren't unhappy with the speech and language therapy I'd been receiving from the Haywood. In fact, Barbara worked with Lois and Amy for a while.

Barbara would lay out a series of pictures and pick out an image, fork for example, and ask me to pick the picture of the object that would be paired with it.

'Seriously?' I thought. 'You must think I'm stupid! strap in, Barbara, I'm gonna smash this.'

I confidently pointed at a spoon.

I knew I should have picked a knife the moment I pointed at it, but I was so keen to show how I could easily do this that I rushed it.

I got the majority right after that, but there were a couple I couldn't find. I wanted to say, "It's a hammer, but I can't find it", but speech was still some time in the future. I desperately wanted Barbara to know my cognitive skills were fine.

The meeting with Barbara ended and Dad asked me what I thought. I spelled out on the letter board "Yes Dad. I think Barbara is the right person to assist me in regaining the ability to talk and I would appreciate the benefit of her expertise."[8]

I didn't have much experience of speech therapists and based my opinion on the fact that I liked her. As it turned out, we'd struck gold and Barbara can be held responsible for my ability to verbally inflict my stupidity on people.

## Temper, Temper

As you can tell from the diary posts I could be a handful and my temper was becoming an issue.

It came to a head when I indicated to Sue that I wanted to go to the toilet. Sue got the help of another nurse to assist with operating the hoist. I was transferred from the bed into the wheelchair and wheeled to the bathroom.

About a metre from the door, I stuck my left foot on the frame so that Sue couldn't wheel me in and angrily indicated that I didn't need the toilet.

---

[8] I probably shortened this to a plain "Yes".

Sue wasn't very impressed; she wheeled me back to my bed and, with the assistance of another nurse, hoisted me back onto my bed.

When Daniel came in for visiting later that day, Sue told him and I got quite a telling off.

I was getting quite a reputation for being difficult, I'd hit Daniel in the face (albeit with the force of being tickled by a feather) I'd seemingly hit Charlotte the physio in the stomach (although that was an accident), and now this latest incident.

Daniel warned me that if I didn't stop this behaviour, I would be transferred to another hospital where the staff are used to dealing with aggressive patients.

I don't know if it was a legitimate threat, but it did the trick. From that point forward I was an angel. When I left there was a big party for me. All the staff were in tears, and they lined up on either side of the corridor to applaud and cheer as I was wheeled out.[9]

---

9 This might be a lie.

## *Chapter 11 – A Refreshing Mint, I'm Wearing a Mask and Wheelies*

```
Speech|Lang 27/3/08

Good session today. Tom had teaspoons of pudding
thick blackcurrant squash + managed these well. Also
went through the oro-meter ex's which Tom completed
well using his full range of movement with
encouragement Tom used the alphabet board very
effectively today and attempted to voice some words
when encouraged.

                              Aimee (SLT Assistant)


27/3/08 14.10

Tom pointed and said "tissue"!

Tom said "fine", "Sue" and "wee".

                                                 Sue
```

Later on that evening Mum, Dad, Laura and Daniel came to visit me. I'd made the odd attempt to speak up to now as the above diary entry states, and I whispered "three" in the early days when correcting Dad on a rugby score.

We congregated in the conservatory as it offered privacy, allowing us to close the door. Mum offered Dad a mint. I had by now progressed to sipping thickened liquids, but certainly couldn't cope with Softmints. I gave a forlorn expression and reached for the packet. "Oh, I'm sorry," said Mum, "That was really insensitive, I'll put them away."

Daniel, my loving older brother, showing great empathy, couldn't resist the moment.

"Ooh, I really fancy a cool refreshing mint, Mom, can I have one please?"

I started to chuckle silently. Laughs at this point were just rhythmic expulsions of air, with no vocal sound whatsoever. Daniel started to laugh at his own hilarity and continued to taunt me.

"Oh no, want a mint do you? Wish you could have one? Bet you wish you could tell me what you really think." and so on.

I'd like to say I was appalled that he would find humour at my current situation. I wasn't. He's a funny fellah anyway, but this was becoming more of a skit, a comedy piece, a bit. My laughs started to gain momentum.

Mum and Dad were laughing as well, their sympathy for my current situation was really quite touching.

Daniel stood up and began accompanying his taunts with antic gestures. My laughs had begun to be audible. My vocal chords were kicking in and I had the urge to use them. So I did.

"F-F-FUCK OFF!"

Laughing, cheering and hugging ensued. Sue came into the conservatory to see what the whoops and laughs were all about.

"He's just spoken!"

"Really? What did he say?"

Everyone looked at everyone else. The silence lengthened.

"Well. Let's just say it wasn't very polite."

Sue put her arm around me and said "You wouldn't say that to me, would you, Tom?"

I smiled sweetly at her.

"Fuck off, Sue."

**I feel the need to interject at this point. Yes, there were hugs, cheers and laughs, but also a few tears. Not only had Tom spoken his first words in months, but they were delivered with the typical (and fortunately uncommon) Shaw humour. It felt as though he'd returned from a long voyage, and we'd missed him terribly.**

**It's also worth expressing our appreciation for the mighty Sue, who had adapted magnificently to our family weirdness and joined in the hilarity at Tom's response.**

You might have noticed I haven't mentioned my tracheostomy since I told you it was fitted after my initial surgery.

It may surprise you to hear that I'm not medically trained. It probably wasn't my responsibility to close my own tracheostomy.

I have a very vague memory of my Mum and Dad coming to visit me at the Q.E. in Birmingham and a nurse coming over to my bed and informing them I had ripped the tracheostomy tube out in my sleep, allowing the opening to close.

The nurse told my parents that my oxygenation levels were fine, and that I was breathing satisfactorily without assistance. They decided to leave me 'tracheostomy free'.

In this case, my somewhat risky action had been taken while asleep, but acting on impulse with no regard for the consequences is something I've been guilty of a number of times in my life.

## An Idiot Doing Idiotic Things

Laura and I decided to go to West Midlands Safari Park. I was in the Nissan - a car I despised; I probably intended to stick red meat all over the car's body and hope the monkeys would rip it apart.

Unfortunately, they were nowhere to be seen, they had all run inside because they didn't want anybody taking photos of them in the Nissan's vicinity.

Giraffes were the last set of animals, wandering amongst the line of cars as we queued to leave.

Food pellets could be purchased from the gift shop, something we weren't aware of. As we reached the giraffe section, we saw people putting the pellets on the roof of their cars. These awesome creatures were walking right up to them to eat the food.

I was jealous, so I said, "I'll stick my hand out like I've got food and when it comes over it'll be close enough to touch."

I opened the window and stuck my arm out as if I was offering food. A giraffe clocked me and started trotting over.

"It's working" I announced excitedly.

The giraffe approached, didn't pause to investigate and swallowed most of my forearm. When it realised there was no plant-based food on the end of this meat stick, it released me.

My arm was dripping in a gallon or so of giraffe spit, which has the viscosity of the thickened drinks that would later become my staple diet. I reached for the sachet of wet wipes to find there was one left.

Wet wipes are tiny.

## Back in Reality

Now I had spoken it was suddenly something I could do whenever I wanted. However, the ability to talk wasn't the positive step in my recovery that you might expect. It shone a light on a number of issues that depressed me.

All I'd heard up to this point was how well I was doing and - as there was nothing I was able to compare to my previous state - I believed these opinions. Now I had evidence that contradicted these claims.

I didn't foresee any issues with my speech, even though my current situation should have been a clue. I continued where I'd left off, assuming talking was simple, requiring nothing other than the ability to open and move my mouth. I had no idea about the complexities of speech; now I was struggling to do it.

Immediately noticeable was my voice. It was so low it was barely audible. There was no expression, no emphasis on certain words. It was difficult to follow what I was saying.

Speech is quite sing-songy; we put emphasis on certain syllables in words. We raise the pitch at the end of sentences to ask questions.

One doesn't realise that expression, tone, mannerisms, annunciation and so on, are just as important to speech as the words. Without these nuances, speech isn't just more difficult to understand, it can be quite boring. It becomes hard to keep people's attention.

I hadn't noticed it when I told Sue to eff off, because I was sidetracked by the elation of people and the fact that I was making people laugh. Now the room was quiet when I spoke, everybody was concentrating on what I had to say, and nobody was laughing.

I hated the sound of my own voice.

I was sure it wasn't mine. I was just borrowing it until my real voice was ready to take over.

I hated how long it took to say something. I wouldn't make any allowances for the fact that my mouth can't move as fast as required. I wouldn't pause or think before I said something, trying to think of the word moments before I said it, and then getting extremely frustrated when I couldn't think of the word I was grasping for.

I could now let Mum, Dad and Laura know what was dominating my thoughts at the time.

"This mask I'm wearing is irritating me."

Refuting my claims meant they would get acquainted with angry Tom.

"Erm, you're not wearing a mask".

It became noticeable that I had an anger issue, although I wouldn't blame this solely on brain surgery. I would go from zero to a hundred in seconds. My temper flicked like a light switch.

"I AM WEARING A MASK!"

They'd reassure me that there was no mask.

"It's under my skin. Just because you can't see it doesn't mean it's not there!"

By now, my temper would be kicking in, partly because of the difficulty in explaining myself. When I spoke, my mouth started filling with saliva. Whoever I was looking at was about to be sprinkled with my frustration too.

I had the natural reaction of swallowing, and this caused another problem. Saliva lacks the consistency of wallpaper paste, unlike the fluids I was receiving at the time. I'd start to cough... and cough and cough... And then I'd cough a bit more.

I had startled my epiglottis, I hadn't told it I intended to swallow, so when I did it was unprepared.[10]

"Are you okay? Have some water."

I gave a thumbs up to say I was okay. I wasn't going to have some water though as I wouldn't be able to swallow it without adding to my coughing fit.

With the fit over and an empty mouth I began to say my highly plausible theory about this mask, but my mouth started to fill with saliva again almost immediately.

I thought it would be quicker to say these words with a gob full of saliva, whilst covering my mouth, rather than initiate another coughing fit.

It just made me even more unintelligible.

My mouth couldn't move quickly enough, and the left side of my jaw was tiring. My speech sounded like Rocky Balboa. Trying to speak quickly meant my top and bottom molars were clashing. I kept biting my tongue on the right side of my mouth.

"Look! Just because you can't see it, doesn't mean it's not there. It's under my skin." I frustratedly repeat and then swallow, followed by coughing.

---

[10] I'm sticking to this theory.

"Your head is not inside a mask, you're not wearing anything".

I am getting very angry, trying to speak even quicker. I tense my body and jam my left foot into the floor.

I'm finding speech incredibly demanding. The effort is enormous, but my audience are too stupid to grasp what I'm trying to say.

This is taking a toll on my body, and these idiots keep disputing what is obvious and making me endure this pain and stress.

I'm tensing my bum cheeks so much it's becoming uncomfortable to sit in my wheelchair. My right leg is aching and to try to get some relief I try to stretch it out as much as I can without kicking people under the table.

"My head feels like it's in a box"

"Your head is not in a box and you're not wearing a mask."

I realise I'm getting nowhere and change the subject.

"I want to go home."

"I know, you can soon."

"I want to go now though."

"But your bedroom's upstairs, how would we get you up there?"

They try to get me away from this completely implausible idea without having to tell me "No!".

"How would we get you into the house? We haven't got the hoist to transfer you".

My answer is along the lines of "You'll manage".

I know it's completely implausible, but in my head if I wasn't in hospital everything would be all right.

Dad asks a question for which I don't have an answer. I loop back.

"I want to go home."

Dad sees this conversation is going nowhere, so he raises his voice slightly to tell me it's not possible just yet. I can tell that he means no, and there's no point in pursuing the subject.

It goes quiet…

"I'm wearing a mask!"

## Wheelies

It was around this period that I got my own wheelchair instead of the hospital's 'extra support' chair. The hospital chair was very large and couldn't be self-propelled. It had to be pushed.

Daniel came with me to Wheelchair Services at Cannock Chase Hospital. I was taken in a transport ambulance, similar to the one I was transferred to the Haywood in, but I wasn't lying in a bed this time, I was sitting in a wheelchair borrowed from the hospital.

Like a bus the seats are on the left and right and there is an aisle between them. Set into the floor are metal tracks; the wheelchair is rolled into place and two belts are secured on a part of the front of the wheelchair and clipped into the metal tracks on the floor. The same process is repeated for the two rear wheels. A belt is wrapped around my waist and then secured in the metal tracks. An electronic ramp is at the back of the ambulance to get me on and off.

Clive from wheelchair services met us and assessed my needs. He asked several questions about my capabilities and what I wanted from the wheelchair.

I expressed my desire for more independence. I said I hadn't used my arms to propel myself yet, but I was sure I could manage it. He recommended a chair and, with the assistance of an occupational therapist and a hoist, I transferred into it to give it a test.

I thought I was pushing both wheels equally, but the chair was turning right. As with my right leg, my right arm was quite happy not to contribute as much as my left. With a little practice, I found a way to compensate; I wasn't doing wheelies and there was no danger I was going to be selected for Team GB, but I managed.

The chair needed a service before delivery. I think this was a Tuesday and Daniel brought it to the Haywood on Friday.

I could now move around the ward without someone pushing me. I still needed to be transferred by the hoist into the wheelchair, but I was getting there - slowly.

# *Chapter 12 – Breathe Better and Twang, Plink, Plonk*

An Idiot Doing Idiotic Things

In 2005 I went abroad for the first time in my life to the Dominican Republic. I wasn't keen on the idea of flying, so for some reason I thought my first flight should be eight hours.

I drove us to Manchester, and my infamous sense of direction was in full effect. As was my habit of refusing to acknowledge I wasn't sure where to go.

After visiting the same wrong part of the airport several times and feeling nauseous from doing multiple circuits of numerous roundabouts, we finally got to the right terminal. We were in danger of missing our flight, so I dumped the car as close to the entrance as possible and ran to check-in.

When we got to the Dominican, my girlfriend spoke to her Dad on the phone, told him where I'd parked the car and he agreed to get my spare keys, drive up to Manchester and park the car in the long stay car park.

We later found out that where I parked was going to cost about twenty quid a day. We were away for fourteen days.

One evening the locals set up market stalls in the grounds of the hotel for the holiday makers to buy trinkets and I saw a friendship bracelet that I wanted.

"How much?" I enquired

"Four dollars."

As I reached for my wallet Laura whispered to me "You're supposed to negotiate."

I stared back blankly and she took over and haggled on my behalf. She got the price down to two dollars and smugly waited for me to pay. I reached into my wallet; I only had a five-dollar note.

"Keep the change."

I walked away to the sound of my girlfriend sighing in disbelief.

## Back in Reality

Impressed by my first meeting with Barbara, we decided to retain her to work on my speech. Fortunately, my first session with her was the day after I'd said my first words. I thought she was going to say "Job done! Ta-ra."

How wrong I was. Now she could see for herself what needed attention, and, well, it's quicker to tell you what *didn't* need attention.

My first words were barely audible and I was speaking at a pitch almost below human hearing. Quite often, if people weren't looking at me and expecting me to talk, then they'd talk over me. They were unaware I was speaking unless they could see my lips moving.

It didn't help that I refused to speak slowly, so my mouth couldn't keep up with what I was saying.

Breath is vital to clear speech, and good breath control is key to sustaining clarity.

My lung capacity was vastly reduced. I could only take in enough air to say a few words before needing another breath. I'd take deep breaths but they'd be jerky and split into multiple stages. I would take in a deep breath, but you wouldn't hear me inhale just once; you'd hear a series of inward gasps. This hadn't been noticeable up to now as I hadn't had to take deep breaths for speech. I tried to take a huge gulp of air, but instead of sounding like Brian Blessed I'd sound like the timid trainee from *fw*. Where did the breath go?

In these early days the word 'dysarthria' was used. I didn't know what this was and had completely forgotten it was spoken about until writing this.

It's where you have difficulty speaking because the muscles you use for speech are weak. It can be caused by conditions that damage your brain or nerves and some medicines. Speech and language therapy can help.

Barbara always made me aware of the importance of breathing correctly. Sitting down and talking is very different to standing and talking. Standing brought my abdominal muscles into play, which is where I should have been breathing from – I was breathing from my chest. She was trying to show me the difference, but I didn't know what this meant; I was breathing, wasn't I?

I took a deep breath and again noticed the multiple gasps.

'She might be onto something you know' I thought.

This intermittent way of breathing was the norm for me back then, but Barbara kept banging this breathing drum, telling me to breathe from the diaphragm.

Lizzie would join Barbara and me to set me up in the standing frame; then, when Lizzie left the hospital, Claire Gu took over.[11]

Once I was standing the physio would step back and Barbara would conduct her therapy session as normal.

We worked on lip and tongue position. I struggled with the 'F' sound. You're supposed to touch your bottom lip with your top teeth. I'm sure I wouldn't have done this, so I probably said "uck off Sue" but it would have been pretty harsh if instead of whooping and cheering, everyone

---

[11] You'll notice that Claire is mentioned an awful lot in this book. You might also notice that they have different surnames. This is because most of the physiotherapy department seemed to be called Claire. To make it even more confusing, two of the Claires had the same initials, which is why there's a Claire G and Claire Gu.

stared at me and asked "pardon? We don't know what you're saying."

Vowel sounds were a challenge. I wasn't making my mouth into the correct shape. I thought I was; I was sure I was doing exactly as the worksheets instructed. I thought Barbara would be amazed by my competency, but she wasn't. She didn't make negative comments, or rap me across the knuckles with a ruler whenever I opened my mouth, but I was hoping to hear gasps of amazement.

Barbara showed me how I should be shaping my mouth. I believed I was mimicking her mouth movements, but she told me the left side of my mouth wasn't moving as much as the right. When I shaped my mouth for an 'O', I was making more of a semicircle than a circle. I especially struggled with vowel sounds when the vowel comes straight after a 'TH' sound. The tip of your tongue has to be between your front teeth, then for a vowel sound your tongue moves to the base of your mouth and your mouth needs to change into a different shape.

Certain words like 'tomorrow' require you to close your lips together to make the 'M' sound. But my jaw would often be tired, and I found that if I skipped this movement, I could save myself the effort. It seemed to have no effect on people's understanding as they relied on the context of my sentence.

I started taking shortcuts. I could save milliseconds by skipping an 'S'. But for words like 'clothes', there was no way round it. As I would prove, talking without moving your tongue is as useful as playing poker without your hands.

There was a lot of emphasis on my swallow. Barbara did constant tests with a teaspoon of water and a small bite of a biscuit to measure its progress. This would make me cough, and then Barbara would measure how much thickener I needed in my drink so that I didn't cough.

Over the duration of my stay my drinks went from containing enough thickener to make them chewable, to such a small amount that when I was discharged and they offered me some to take home with me, I decided I would be okay without it.

# Twang, Plink, Plonk

31.3.08

```
Spoke to Brian, he has locked Tom's guitar in the
cupboard thus it is safe.
```

                                                        Sue

Brian was the Activities Coordinator. He was basically tasked with keeping everyone's morale up by playing games and quizzes, and in my case, teaching me to play guitar again.

He was probably the most incredible guitarist I'd ever met. He wasn't one of these Eddie Van Halen types who moves around the fretboard like lightning, trying to hit as many strings as he can within a second. I think that sounds awful, I prefer the Tommy Emmanuel type.

Brian played in bands and sometimes kept his guitar at the Haywood. I was immediately impressed by his playing. I got chatting to him and it turned out he was a big music fan. 'Okay,' I thought to myself, 'playing the guitar and being a music fan are two big ticks'. We talked about Pink Floyd. He said he wasn't a big fan, but his favourite Pink Floyd album was *Animals.* JACKPOT! This admission convinced me he was a genuine music buff. Most people name *Dark Side of the Moon*, *Wish You Were Here* or *The Wall* as their favourite Floyd album, but he'd named my favourite.

I've never been a good guitarist and didn't play in bands or in public, but I loved it. My Dad is pretty good, and as a result there were always a few guitars knocking around the house. I hadn't shown any particular interest in playing; on the odd occasion we'd have a bit of a jam session with Dad and Daniel on guitar and Adam on keyboards or guitar. Or penny whistle. Or saxophone, bassoon, harp, trumpet, kazoo, comb (basically anything). I would just sit and watch with my Mum.

As I got older, I became heavily into Pink Floyd, who are also one of my Dad's favourite bands. He had a Giannini acoustic, which I loved and started trying to play. Dad showed me the basics and then I would go away and teach myself. I always had my Dad or Daniel to show me things if I needed help. They would both finger-pick more than strum, which meant I learnt that talent pretty quickly. It became my favourite pastime, and I would always grab the guitar if there was one in the vicinity.

Back in 2005, I was on holiday in Scotland with my parents and my girlfriend. We happened by a music shop that was closing down. There was a gorgeous purple semi-acoustic guitar which I fell in love with. I had a little play on it but couldn't play much at this stage, so Dad gave it a good test. It was a Brunswick; not an expensive brand, but he was of the opinion it was a genuine bargain.

Admittedly, Brunswick guitars don't have the greatest reputation, but this one was genuinely pretty good. I remember it very fondly.

It was my first guitar!
And it was semi acoustic so I could plug it in!
And it was purple!

I didn't have an amplifier as that might have given people the impression I thought I was quite good, so I just plugged it into my computer speakers.

For now, I decided against buying it and Dad gave it back to the owner of the shop.

We went to a nearby beach. I questioned whether I should have bought it.

"They only wanted a hundred pounds," I said.

"You should get it," was the general consensus.

I think this is what they said; I only heard "you sh-" as I was already on my way.

I ran back to the shop in the pouring rain, praying that it would still be open when I got there. The closed sign was visible through the glass panel of the door, but in desperation I pulled the handle. It opened and the doorbell rang as I stepped in, escaping from the downpour outside. The startled shop attendant looked up from the magazine she was reading and saw me creating a puddle on the floor.

She went into the back and returned holding a towel, handing it to me and saying "you're soaking wet!".

"Is it raining? I hadn't noticed."

I held out the hundred pounds. She took it and handed me a guitar case with the guitar already in it.

"I knew you'd be back," she said with a smile on her face.[12]

I went back to the beach and played the same three songs repeatedly. And badly.

Back to the hospital…

Now able to talk, my first request was "Can you bring my guitar in?" As seemed to be a constant theme, I didn't consider if I would even be able to play it any more; I was just thinking about playing it like I used to.

The guitar was placed on my lap and immediately I noticed a problem: I couldn't see the front of the guitar and the arms of the chair meant that they were stopping it from sitting close to me. I was sitting with my back against the backrest, because I struggled to sit up unsupported.

I felt I could perch on the edge of the seat if I planted my feet into the floor to stop me from falling forward. I shuffled forward in the wheelchair, but my now unsupported torso was waving from side to side like a tree

---

[12] This really happened. Richard Curtis has been on the phone constantly, begging me to let him make a film of it.

in a breeze. Fortunately, the arms of the wheelchair were preventing me from falling to the left or right. To get more stability I jammed my left foot into the floor and tensed my body.

I held the neck with my left hand and hooked my right arm over the body. I held the plectrum as one is meant to - a small part of the plectrum between the index finger and thumb, but my hand did its usual cat squirm and I dropped it. It was picked up and handed back to me. I held it differently this time, but I had to hold so much of it that there was only a tiny point of the plectrum visible through my fingers.

As the left hand – my more stable hand - is responsible for fingering chords, I wasn't too worried about its accuracy. But though it didn't shake, I couldn't land my fingers on specific strings. I'd aim for the third string but land on the second, so I'd try again and hit the fourth. Then I couldn't press my fingers down properly and they were sometimes spanning across other strings, so it sounded awful when I strummed. I tried to stand my fingers on end so just the fingertips were touching the string, but my hand would start shaking violently.

So much for my good hand!

I couldn't judge the strength with which I was strumming the strings with my right hand, and I couldn't strum with any rhythm. I'd try not to strum too hard and would then miss the strings altogether. I was forever dropping the plectrum either on the floor or into the sound-hole. I tried finger-picking, as maybe that would be easier, but it was much, much harder; my fingers moved slowly and I certainly hadn't got the dexterity and precision to play a specific string with a specific finger. The lack of feeling meant I couldn't tell how hard I was pulling; it was a wonder I didn't pull the string clean off.

My mood plummeted again. I went into this visit excited I was going to get to play my guitar again. I did say to myself that I wouldn't be able to play like I used to, but with some practice I would get there. Suddenly I was faced with the reality that I wasn't going to be able to play at all.

This hit me hard. I could barely even hold the thing. It was heartbreaking. I tried my best not to show this emotion on the outside. I asked Dad to take the guitar off me and he propped it up on the chair. I was clearly upset and was told I just needed to practise. I didn't share the optimism; I tried to explain that it wasn't a lack of practice, it was a lack of physical ability.

This was another dose of reality, and it was really starting to get me down. Even though I wasn't keeping a mental list of things wrong with me, each dose of reality was like another kick in the teeth I didn't expect. I was starting to expect it constantly though. I began thinking I couldn't do *anything*.

This would have been a good time to ask "Just what is wrong with me, and will I ever get better?" Up to this point I'd always thought I would recover fully and get back to how I was - after all that is what I'd been told at the start. The goalposts had moved though. I knew that when I went home, I was going to have to rest up, but up to this point I thought that meant I would have weeks or months of noodling on the guitar. I could quite happily accept that. Now I realised that wasn't going to be possible.

# *Chapter 13 - Work, Hyoscine patches and What's That noise*

### An Idiot Doing Idiotic Things

It's 2006 and I'm going to see my first client since becoming self-employed. He had given me directions, but unfortunately there were certain roads I had to take, turns I had to make, roundabouts I had to negotiate.

This was back in the days when sat-nav was only fitted in the most luxurious of cars and smartphones were in their infancy.

I'm an idiot, so should have known better.

I got lost.

I was speeding up the A34 – already late – and took the wrong exit from a roundabout. Fortunately, there was another roundabout straight after. I sped around that and returned to take the correct exit on the first roundabout.

A week later I received a letter telling me I'd been caught speeding. Twice. I was going to receive two fines of sixty pounds and six penalty points. The two fines were within a minute of each other.

I wrote back to them saying surely this was a mistake. They're trying to penalise me twice for the same offence.

I sent the letter and awaited an apology.

Instead, I received a reply with two photographs and a covering letter, saying I'm an idiot (I'm paraphrasing).

The first photo was the rear of my car; the second photo was my car from the front and showed me peering over the steering wheel. There's a speed camera on the central reservation, about 100 yards from the roundabout that caught me in both directions. The only upside to this is that I'd never have believed that bloody awful Nissan could accelerate that fast.

## Back in Reality

Brian was at the Haywood Monday to Friday and we would usually play chess. I only ever managed to beat him once in the dozens of games we played - the last game we played hours before I was discharged. Coincidence?

This sentimentality wasn't fooling me because he seemed to have taken great delight when he beat me convincingly every time in the past, saying "You'll never beat me".

When I passed him on the ward he would ask, "Do you want a game of chess?" Straight away he'd continue, "No you're working..."

I should explain the "working" comment.

My pre-tumour work had been developing web applications. I'd built my own system that allowed customers to manage their own content.

Adam told me that my cousin Joe wanted to be able to update his website and upload videos. He was probably just making conversation, but I seized on it; this was something I could still do. I saw the opportunity to finally have a win.

"I can build that for him. I'll put it in my content management system."

While this offer was working its way through to Joe, I decided to get back on the horse with web coding.

I now had Dad's laptop for watching DVDs, as my portable DVD player had broken a few weeks earlier. Daniel organised a Vodafone dongle for Internet access.

I was now able to get back to my work of developing websites, just a few months after lying unconscious in the Intensive Care Unit.

Only working with one eye really slowed me down. I couldn't see half of the screen unless I was looking at it through my left eye. My neck ached from constantly turning my head to see all of the screen and looking down to see the keys.

At least my ability to use a mouse had improved since my attempts at the Q.E. I wasn't knocking it repeatedly onto the floor. The hand splints – despite my reluctance to wear them for any length of time – had worked. I was able to grab and hold the mouse. I had no peripheral vision though, I couldn't see how close the mouse was to the edge of the desk.

Preparing the system for Joe's use seemed an insurmountable amount of work. I couldn't progress at the speed I needed to get on top of it.

I employed my trusty trick of digging my foot into the floor and tensing my body to give me more stability. I was feeling incredibly stressed and under a lot of pressure. Rather than admit defeat - which would mean admitting I was now incapable - I ploughed on.

I needed to work faster, but I was running out of tricks. I excluded my right hand from the process, so that I wasn't wasting so much time deleting letters I'd typed by mistake.

I still wasn't going quick enough. I spent every spare moment in the daily routine working. When all the other patients were relaxing, I'd be working. I hated it.

Visiting became an inconvenience because that was time spent not working. When my family visited, I painted a smile on my face and told them it was good to be able to get back to normality. I cancelled the daytime visits from Daniel on the weekend so I could spend the time working.

After I'd been struggling with this for a while, Adam told me not to worry as Joe had sorted it. I was relieved and pleased I'd managed to disguise the fact I couldn't do the job any more – well I believed that.

## Hyoscine patch

```
Doctor   has   prescribed   some   patches   which   will
hopefully reduce the amount of saliva produced.
                                                        Sue
```

Talking had led to my mouth constantly producing saliva. This happened even during the day when I wasn't talking much. And I was frequently forgetting to swallow. Most of my tee-shirts were stained from drool that had remnants of the thickener.

I've mentioned before that swallowing required a conscious action that I couldn't always manage without coughing. Dribbling was more reliable - I didn't have saliva in my mouth and I didn't cough. I realised this wasn't a permanent solution.

I fired the Sue Signal into the sky.

Sue described my problem to the doctor, who prescribed a Hyoscine Patch. It's used for people who suffer from travel sickness and may be used to reduce the production of saliva after major surgery.

I suspect it didn't do anything other than remind me to swallow simply by its presence behind my ear but, placebo or not, the dribbling stopped.

## What's That Noise

I sometimes heard a rushing wind noise in my head. It wasn't constant, but it was alarming. When wearing headphones, I noticed that sound in my right ear was muffled.

As I was in a hospital surrounded by doctors and nurses I thought I may as well share my concerns.

I fired the Sue Signal into the sky, but she didn't respond. Jo, however, did. I now had an Alice signal, a Sue signal and a Jo signal. This was starting to get complicated.

A nurse called Lee took me to the Ear Nose and Throat (ENT) clinic, which was in the same hospital. I was equipped with a pair of headphones and a buzzer the shape and size of a lipstick. A sound was played in each ear, starting quietly and getting louder. I had to press the button when I heard the sound.

I passed this test "without any problems to worry about" but I'd passed tests "without any problems" before, so this filled me with little confidence.

I spoke to Jo and explained my concerns. I made sure I spoke very slowly to her, to be sure I was very clear, and nothing could be misunderstood.

I told Jo I was concerned they'd misunderstood me and as a result were testing for something different.

25|4|08

```
I had a look in Tom's medical notes regarding his ENT
appointment yesterday. What Tom was saying yesterday
was correct – the sensory-neuro hearing loss in his
right ear is not severe enough to warrant a hearing
aid.

With regard to the request sent for Tom to attend an
appointment at Edgbaston Dr Bandi is in the process
of talking with Dr Ward as to whether or not Tom
should attend this – we don't know the outcome but
we will ask Dr Bandi next time he's on the ward.

Hope this is ok!

                                    Jo (staff nurse)
```

# *Chapter 14 - Sad Eyes, Sociable Tom and Closed Eyes*

### An Idiot Doing Idiotic Things

It was a friend's twenty-first birthday. His girlfriend had arranged for a group of us to go to an indoor go kart track. Two of my friends were saying the winner would be one of them as they had done it before.

I'd never been karting before, but these two couldn't even drive. Not taking into account my previous driving mishaps I thought 'You two can't even drive, I'm going to destroy you.'

The competitive side of me had taken over, and when I'm in charge of a go-kart, it's not going to end well.

I didn't want to alert them of my intentions though as that might make me a marked man.

We got onto the track and the three of us were having a competitive race. I was in third though. I couldn't get in front of either of them and wasn't really getting any closer. As I passed the start/finish line there was a lap time electronic board and I was second on it behind the leader of the race.

As it seemed fairly likely I wasn't going to win, or come second, I decided I was going to at least get the fastest lap. I went far quicker than the capabilities of the go-kart, in my quest. I got to the third corner, barely broke and ploughed into the tyre wall. I hit the tires so hard I raised out of the seat only to be held down by my legs hitting the steering wheel.

A handy little safety feature!

The steward screamed at me to slow down before dragging the rear of the kart back onto the track. I'd given myself a bit of a scare, but I was fifth now. There had been no consequences to my idiocy plus I now knew there were tyre walls and this ingenious safety measure.

I sped off.

I finished fourth and got the third fastest lap.

## Back in Reality

I was pretty down at this point. Things were getting on top of me. Now I was getting better, I was constantly finding out that I couldn't do things as well as I used to, or at all.

I'd had a very positive moment in saying my first words, but this seemed to have paved the way for various emotions that I was bottling up. When I had visitors, I would give the impression that everything was fine. This wasn't a conscious effort to hide the truth; for the few hours they visited each day I genuinely was fine. I had people to talk to. My mind was occupied.

I didn't burden them with my thoughts because at that moment I had forgotten all about them.

When Daniel visited, he would bring football and boxing DVD's and we'd generally just pass the time having a laugh.

For the evening visiting we would play card games or the Guess the Intro board game. When they left, I'd go to bed, watch a bit of a film and then go to sleep. I'd be shattered because the days would start at seven-thirty (I don't do early mornings).

During the days it was the opposite - and I've only got myself to blame as it shouldn't have been. If there was ever an environment to get you back into social situations, it was this one. I now regret how I spent my time at the Haywood; I barely spoke to anyone, and I would generally sit at my computer with my headphones on, watching films.

Growing up, I was a fairly sociable kid, but then I was in an environment where I couldn't help be sociable. I grew up on an estate where there were lots of kids all around my age; we would play football, rounders, French cricket, killer spray, kerby (I won't go on as some of these names won't mean anything to you).

Time passed and people weren't playing games on the estate any more. They were hanging around with other friends they met at school. I was the only one that went to a different school.

As I got older, people my age were drinking, smoking and spending time with girls. This seemed like a natural progression for them. They seemed to be singing from a hymn sheet I hadn't received.

I became more and more withdrawn, spending a lot of time on my own and on the computer. I didn't feel ousted or excluded; I was doing what I wanted to do. I didn't say anything to anyone because I didn't have anything to complain about. I had friends, but I saw them less and less.

On the first day back in my last year of school, everybody was walking to their first lesson after morning registration. As I walked between the buildings, I suddenly vomited by a wall. I didn't feel particularly ill, but went to the medical room anyway and took the rest of the day off.

As we pulled up outside school the next day, I started to get a stomach pain and a nauseous feeling. It was sudden and I'd felt fine for the rest of the short trip. I told my Dad, who'd given me a lift, and he assured me I'd be fine when I went in.

I wasn't.

I started to have issues with going to school from this point forward. I would retch over the kitchen sink before I walked out of the door. It was part of my morning routine; wake up, get washed, have breakfast, retch. I wouldn't feel well during my time at school and would spend lessons with my head resting on my folded arms on the desk in lessons. I'd spend break times on my own.

My parents tried to find out what was wrong with me, but I wouldn't tell them because I didn't think there was anything wrong.

It was Daniel who managed to get me to open up. He'd moved out by this time and had called round. I was alone in the living room, playing computer games. Mum was upstairs doing the ironing.

He told me Mum and Dad were worried about me and urged me to open up. I explained that I wasn't intentionally not saying anything, I just had nothing to say. I can't remember what was said from there, but at least he persuaded me to speak to my parents.

I can't remember what I told them, but Mum ended up taking me to the doctors, so I guess I made some sense.

I'm not sure if I explained myself properly to the doctor, but I told him about my nausea, both before and during school. By this time I'd also stopped going out in the evening.

My memory is that the doctor prescribed beta-blockers, though as they were chewable and tasted sweet, I now question whether I'm right.

While walking between classes at school, I took out the tube to dose myself. My friend noticed and asked me what it was. As I didn't really know myself, I said, "I get kind of nervous which makes me feel a bit ill. I have some of these sweets and I feel better."

I knew this wasn't very convincing as I heard myself say it, so I played it down.

The beta blockers, if that's what they were, were useless, I may as well have been taking Tic Tacs.

We would regularly go to Rowley Park to play Football, but I was having problems just doing this.

Three of us were chatting on the tennis court and I tried to explain my issues, but what had sounded fine in my head sounded silly when saying it to other people.

I tried to explain I'd had an issue coming here today; I told them about the dry retching. To me it sounded inane, and I assumed they were thinking the same. I downplayed it, made out like it wasn't a big deal and turned attention to something else.

The rest of my last year at school was pretty miserable. I became more and more of a loner and soon I didn't really have any friends. I'd opened up a line of communication with my parents, but I still wasn't explaining it properly.

I knew I had problems going out and didn't have any friends, but at home I could pass the time on my

PlayStation and avoid thinking about it. I'd deal with school tomorrow.

I employed my usual attitude of ignoring the problem and just hoping it would go away.

As the GCSE exams came closer, my schoolmates would revise together, but I'd revise on my own. I didn't think I was missing out on anything because I'd always been on my own up to this point anyway. A few gatherings were organised at weekends, which somehow I got invited to. I'd have every intention of going, but on the day of the gathering, I'd feel physically sick and phone to pull out. I'm sure this became an expected phone call, and slowly the invitations dried up. I was just glad I'd got out of it.

In between school and college, I was prescribed Fluoxetine because the doctor concluded I was 'depressed'. This was back in the days before there was the current focus on mental health; a lot of things seemed to fall under the general term 'depression'. I'm not sure medication would be prescribed before counselling nowadays, but Fluoxetine seemed to be a wonder drug. I was able to go anywhere without any problems.

I took Fluoxetine right up until my surgery. Then I had a few months off as it wasn't a necessary drug to keep me alive directly after brain surgery. It was prescribed again shortly after I arrived at the Haywood, as it became clear I wasn't handling things particularly well.

At some point before I began to speak again, I had a bit of an episode where I was quite agitated and clearly distressed. It was decided to take me off Fluoxetine and put me on to Sertraline, an alternative antidepressant. I still take Setraline to this day.

## Sociable Tom

Now that I was able to talk, I thought I would take advantage of this reacquired ability to see if I could make some friends.

I saw two patients chatting in the corridor - Pete and a lady whose name I can't remember.

'They'll do' I thought.

I'm uneasy approaching people, always have been. I've very rarely approached somebody I don't know on my own. I'm nearly always with somebody I know. Their presence gives me confidence, an assurance that not everybody thinks I'm a moron.

Even if I know the people I'm approaching, I assume they'll crack a joke and say something derogatory about me under their breath.

Now that I'm in a wheelchair it takes me longer to approach somebody, which gives me even more time to convince myself they don't want to talk to me. My self-confidence, already low, had fallen even further.

Afraid I wouldn't think of anything to say when I got there, I started writing a script in my head. I planned the conversation, what I would say and what they would say back. I didn't consider that they wouldn't have this script and wouldn't answer the way I'd planned.

I wanted to try and hide my speech problems and started stressing about making sure this went perfectly. I'd swallow before I spoke, which involved letting my epiglottis know it should be prepared. I'd take a breath before I spoke to hide my intermittent breathing. I'd reply with short answers so that I didn't have to swallow or take a breath mid-sentence.

But I knew that no matter how much I choreographed this dance, I couldn't do anything about how I sounded. My words were all going to come out on one tone. I knew I couldn't put emphasis or stress on parts of words or change the volume.

It's possible I was over-thinking this.

I enter the conversation already thinking they don't want me here. I immediately start rushing so that I can finish this conversation as quickly as possible and inflict my presence on them for as little time as possible.

I greet them and they respond the way I planned. Clearly this is an indication of my talent for writing scripts.

Encouraged, I roll out my prepared question.[13] They don't reply as I rehearsed. Now I'm thrown. I try to think of an answer that's easy to say, doesn't drench them in spit, doesn't require me to swallow mid-sentence and won't need me to take an extra breath.

My mouth does fill up and I swallow without informing my epiglottis. I cough. And cough. And cough.

"Are you ok?"

---

[13] I can't remember what it was.

I can't speak and cough, so I nod while covering my mouth. I take advantage of a momentary lull and say whatever ad lib has come into my head, then I cough a bit more.

I keep my hand over my mouth as it's filling with saliva again and I don't want to spit on them.

I look like an extra from the Walking Dead, I've got surgical tape over my glasses lens and a Hyoscine patch stuck behind my ear with a brown plaster covering it. I probably have dribble down my front.

I'm sure they want rid of me, so I speak quickly. My body tenses and I jam my left leg into the ground. I don't make much sense and they try their best to interpret what I've said.

It's fair to say the conversation isn't flowing as I'd imagined. I just want to get back to my bed, put my headphones on and be on my own.

It should never have been easier to make friends. We're all in hospital, in a similar situation, and we all have a medical problem. That's a very easy ice-breaker, something I already know we have in common.

I changed from the Jo signal back to the Sue Signal and confided in her. This was always stress-free. I didn't feel I had to plan these conversations; she was already aware of my speech problems. I felt comfortable ad-libbing with her.

```
21.4.08
Lesley Stuart (psychologist) will come and see Tom.
Tom says his mood's the same today. Any more issues
see staff cause I will not see you for one week.
                                         Take care Sue
```

## Closed Eyes

I started seeing a clinical psychologist around the rehab unit, but something tipped me off that this wasn't Lesley. I think it was his beard.

He clearly hadn't come to see me as he was trying to strike up a conversation with anybody who would talk to him. He would come up to people while they were in the middle of an activity with Brian, or he would walk around the wards approaching people on their beds and then move onto the next as though he was a cold caller being abruptly dismissed.

I didn't hear any of these conversations, but I got the impression he was about as welcome as somebody stopping you in a mall to ask your opinions on detergent.

He continued this until he fixed his sights on me. I'm not very good at being intentionally rude. Unintentionally rude on the other hand…

He came over to my bed, where I was watching a film with the headphones on.

"And who do you support?" he said.

"Sorry?" I responded, removing the headphones.

"And who do you support?" he said condescendingly, speaking slowly and over-enunciating.

"Erm, Sheffield Wednesday…"

"I don't really follow football. I don't know if they're good or not."

I don't remember the rest of the conversation, but he used it to assess my mental health.

I had a meeting with him, my parents, Daniel and Laura. We were in the conservatory, and he sat at the head of the table.

Eyes closed, he proceeded to share his findings after 'assessing' me. Closing his eyes seemed to be as vital to speech as moving his lips. Opening them again didn't seem to be as fundamental, as he wouldn't do this for a few seconds. It was as if he was enjoying music that we couldn't hear.

Lost in his secret symphony, he said "Thomas isn't depressed as we had a chat and he said he wasn't."

He clearly believed he was giving the definitive diagnosis of my mental health. I think he expected to open his eyes to see admiring, teary-eyed faces looking back at him.

'Really?' I thought. 'Your job must be a doddle if you just need to ask the patient for their own diagnosis'.

I can guarantee that I'd said I wasn't depressed because if I had said "Yes, I am depressed," he would have asked me further questions which I preferred to avoid.

I can appreciate that I'd have been a tricky patient to diagnose because I'd have tried to pretend everything was fine. But I doubt if that's uncommon. Surely a psychiatrist should be able to sense that the twenty-five-year-old, in hospital, recovering from brain surgery, unable to walk and not able to talk very well might be a bit fed up?

```
Hi
I spoke to Tom today about how he is feeling, his
sense of his progress and his interests/activities.
He showed me his Greenwing DVDs, he's occupying
himself with these today and appreciates the humour.
In terms of [unreadable] feelings he has felt
[unreadable] and upset but feels he is now able to
take a constructive view and believes he is
[unreadable] progress in his rehab. He said he is
willing to speak to me again! Normally visit the unit
Mondays & Thursdays.
                                            Michael
```

(There are unreadable words in this diary entry)

I think he was sharing some more pearls of wisdom with his eyes closed when I started laughing hysterically, pointed at the window and shouted "FAT PIGEON".

He opened his eyes to see a not particularly rotund pigeon had landed outside, it wasn't fat but it was bigger than your average pigeon and I thought pointing out its presence was important enough to interrupt the 'psychiatrist'.

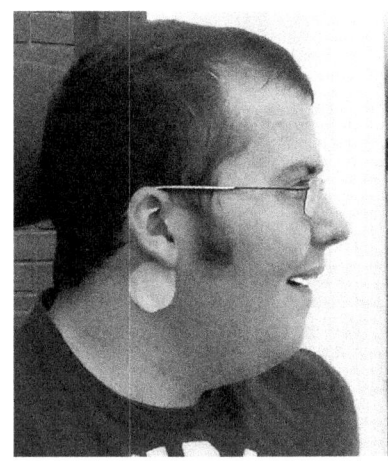

"FAT PIGEON!" I repeated and collapsed in fits of laughter. It was infectious, and everybody apart from Michael joined in.

He looked at us, puzzled. I imagine he was thinking, 'See, he's not depressed because he's laughing', while metaphorically giving himself a pat on the back.

I don't recall having any further dealings with this highly qualified professional after this.

I didn't need to be intentionally rude and make up a believable excuse as to why I couldn't see him anymore. He didn't approach me again. I clearly wasn't depressed, and his work was done.

# *Chapter 15 - It's Not Our Fault and The Zutons*

### An Idiot Doing Idiotic Things

Laura and I were going to stay with Daniel and his girlfriend for the night.

We were going to go to a comedy club. I remember saying to Laura on the morning of our departure "The comic better not say anything about my weight", as I stretched the medium sized shirt over my large torso.

The four of us stopped at a pub on the way which had a bar billiards table.

I'd never seen a bar billiards table and suggested we go to another pub that didn't have holes in the pool table.

We stayed.

I lost and we headed to the comedy club.

The first comic came on and wasn't particularly funny. I think he agreed, and turned his attention to the audience. What better way to get a laugh than to make fun of me.

"You look like you've enjoyed a few Christmases."

"What's your name?" He asked me.

I'm sure my reply had him seriously considering his comedic career.

"I'm not telling you".

Boom!

That told him.

## Back in Reality

We had a meeting with a partner from the doctor's surgery and a woman whose role I'm not sure of.

My parents, girlfriend and Daniel were present.

I can't remember much at all from this meeting as it didn't seem very important at the time, in fact it was a hassle; this was keeping me from my busy day of watching films. As to how we came to be having this meeting, I'll hand over to Dad.

**The repeated poor diagnoses, sketchy examinations, delays and general inefficiency of the local doctors' surgery may or may not have allowed Tom's condition to worsen. What is undeniable is that they failed to respond adequately to a life-threatening condition. When the need for an MRI scan was agreed, the referring doctor went on holiday without ordering it.**

**Concerned that this behaviour might put other patients at risk, I lodged an official complaint. A meeting ensued at which the practice's senior partner and a colleague came to the Haywood for a meeting...**

It's been sixteen years since this meeting, so my memories aren't detailed, but the main elements are reasonably clear. I understood that this was a review to determine if they were at fault. As was expected, they immediately went on the defensive and repeatedly stated guidelines that, in their eyes, exonerated them.

Beyond a simple, "hello", they barely acknowledged my arrival in the room. I felt some expression of sympathy or at least an enquiry about my health might have been appropriate.

Without any such pleasantries, the business of the meeting began. They made their position clear from the start: they weren't at fault. They explained that their required reaction time for non-urgent cases was six weeks.

But this was urgent, we protested.

"Yes, but we didn't know that at the time."

It was pointed out to them that, when a healthy man in his early twenties is suffering disabling head pain and nausea, it should be clear that timely investigation is required.

They countered by referring to notes saying that the patient was suffering from headaches. Examination of the retinas didn't show any adverse symptoms, so there was no urgency.

"But I made it very clear that these weren't headaches," I said. "They were intense head pains."

"Yes, but the system is electronic, and there's no category for that, so we recorded a headache."

Is it just me, or is this a ludicrous argument? If we rely on computer forms – that are self-evidently incomplete – to diagnose symptoms, what's the point of doctors?

Leaving that aside, the practice had significantly delayed diagnosis because a doctor went on holiday. Another doctor recommended I see a dentist. A further suggestion was to sleep on one pillow. As far as I know, none of this was recorded in the notes.[14]

The meeting ended inconclusively.

**We pursued the complaint without success. Some weeks later, I met with the senior partner in his office. He showed that the case (based**

---

[14] Probably because that option was missing too.

entirely on the practice's own notes) had been reviewed (at an inquiry to which we were not invited) and a decision reached that no failure had occurred.

I was furious but, advised that no further action could be taken, was forced to accept the verdict. I did, however, say to the doctor, "There's no one else in this room. We both know what really happened here. If you acknowledge that fact, privately, and assure me that steps have been taken to ensure it doesn't happen again, we'll consider the matter closed."

He nodded, and with that I had to be content.

# The Zutons

```
28/5/08

We did some sitting balance today & helped Tom tilt
his pelvis. Tom then did 3 stands with us, he needed
quite a lot of prompting which worried Tom as he only
has 4 weeks to the Zutons, so we are going to work
hard with Tom on getting good safe transfers.
```

Lydia

Physio

I'd seen The Zutons once before in Preston, with about one hundred other people in a shopping mall. That was a few years earlier and they were playing to bigger audiences now.

They'd be performing at Cannock Chase in four weeks on June 28th. Laura knew I liked them and asked the nurses if I'd be allowed out of the hospital to go and see them. They agreed that this would be a great goal to aim for and said yes.

I'd now progressed to a turntable for transferring to and from the wheelchair without the need for a hoist. Medically it's referred to as a turner, but in the ward, it was known, inevitably as Tina.

Tina was a great bit of kit that only required one nurse to operate.[15] It had a spinning plate that I'd stand on, and a handle about four feet tall. I would pull myself up, and the nurse would turn me ninety degrees so that I could sit down in my wheelchair.

I was still unsteady on my feet, and it had to be turned very slowly, as any jolt would have me toppling sideways. I was holding myself up by the handlebars rather than supporting my weight through my legs, but it was progress.

As I wouldn't have this piece of kit with me at the gig, I would need to master a step transfer.

I changed the Sue Signal to the Physio Signal and summoned help.

They had four weeks to whip me into shape and train me for a real-world situation. The physios weren't going to be there to catch me if I started to topple, the only thing that was going to stop my fall was the ground.

---

[15] Oh, grow up!

29|5|08 - Physio/OT

Washing and dressing practice. Tom's sitting balance improved today compared to previous sessions. Able to maintain balance at times whilst carrying out activities which he hasn't been able to do for before. Told Tom he should be very pleased with this!

Tom has a goatee at his request. Practiced standing transfers + stepping around - much better than yesterday. Will continue to practice.

Alice

I found the sessions quite demoralising at first.

A step transfer basically uses a person instead of the turner. It required me to put my arms on the physio's shoulders, them putting their hands on my shoulders/forearms and me stepping ninety degrees so that the wheelchair was behind me. Then I'd bend my knees, gently sit down and lean back, rather than just falling and expecting the backrest to stop me.

Transferring up to now hadn't relied on much - or any input - from me. Until recently I had been carried like a baby in the hoist.

For this transfer, my arms should have been resting on the physio's shoulders for balance only, and my legs supporting my weight. I thought I was doing this, but the handprints on her shoulder suggested differently.

I couldn't step very far to the side with my right leg, I could only reach a very short distance. A ninety-degree turn that could have been completed in one step was taking three.

My centre of gravity was very narrow. If I took big steps, I'd begin to topple and the physio would have to push against the direction I was falling.

Up to now I don't think I'd been putting in as much effort as I could have been. I wasn't sure what the end goal was. I just had to do the best I could and improve as much as I could.

For once though, I was asking questions rather than just assuming I was doing what was asked. Sessions were going well, I felt I had something to achieve, and I was clear on what that was. My stepping improved rapidly. I still had to take multiple steps as my right leg couldn't reach far, but as long as I took my time and didn't stretch too far, I nailed it every time.

After four weeks of practising for what would be about ten seconds out of the wheelchair, I was ready. I was going to a gig!

I put on my Zutons tee-shirt and headed out. The nurses set a midnight curfew and gave me strict instructions not to have alcohol.

I was extremely excited. I thought about the last gig I'd been to - Ian Brown in Birmingham. That was quite a happy memory, but – as with everything at the time – I wasn't thinking about how things would be now. I massively underestimated how different they'd turn out.

A people carrier taxi with my girlfriend, one of her friends and two cousins arrived at the hospital to pick me up. A nurse helped me transfer from the wheelchair into the taxi using the turner and then took it back into the hospital.

It was one of those people-carrier taxis with two rows of forward-facing seats in the back. My seat was beside the door, it was quite a step up, but I had no problem.

The taxi started moving, sounding as though a box of nuts and bolts had been emptied inside the car. It rattled and squeaked, and every stone that we ran over sounded as though the thing was about to collapse around us. There was so much road noise I thought the windows were open. People were practically shouting to communicate.

Conversation was moving quite quickly. I was used to situations where usually only one person was talking, and there wasn't any environmental noise. Here, people were butting in or finishing each other's sentences.

I was struggling immediately. I was shouting to be heard. I was barely saying one word before needing another breath. If I paused to take a breath somebody would start talking, not realising that I hadn't finished. My mouth would fill with saliva, and having to talk so loud meant that the seat in front of me was going to get drenched. I would try to swallow quickly, determined to finish my sentence, but I would cough. And cough. And cough.

I was sitting facing forwards so nobody could see me. I didn't dare turn in my seat as I needed to lean back against the chair.

All I had to rely on was my voice.

My speech is difficult to hear and people who aren't looking at me, or expecting me to speak, would talk over me.

Expression, tone and mannerisms are just as important as speech when communicating. A question can be asked just by the way stress is put on certain words or by speaking slightly higher at the end of a sentence.

We tend to accompany what we're saying with actions. Even if not heard clearly, it can be interpreted what's been said by the accompanying mannerisms.

I found myself having to say, "That was a question" when I realised people weren't answering me. I was having to say, "That was a joke" or laugh at the end of what I said to show I was joking. This was intended to prompt people to laugh.

I knew they weren't laughing because they were amused, they were laughing because I'd prompted them. Saying something funny is often only funny because of the way you say it.

I tried to fit in. I didn't want to get in the way of the flow of the conversation. I didn't want people to have to make allowances for the sick person.

I was trying to speak quickly. I was jamming my foot into the floor and tensing my body. My right arm and right leg were hurting. I was finding this whole process frustrating and physically tiring.

I stopped trying to join in, hoping to alleviate the tension in my body. I was going to be in my wheelchair for many hours and my right leg was already hurting.

We arrived ridiculously early, so I was able to get out of the taxi without anybody watching me. I hadn't been bothered by how others saw me up to this point. I hadn't thought about it. I hadn't even looked in a mirror. I was a patient in a hospital surrounded by other patients. It was an image-free zone. I suddenly felt incredibly self-conscious and embarrassed. Thankfully, there weren't many people around.

I felt deep regret at that point. I used to be in great shape, I'd gone from years of constant exercise to years of no exercise and eating and drinking anything and everything. Why didn't I just relax the exercise regime, but still maintain some level of fitness?

Why did I stop it all together?

The taxi driver got out and stood by us as he was wary that my girlfriend alone was supporting me. Her friend and cousins were poised, ready to stop me if I started toppling. They needn't have worried because my step transfer was flawless. I carefully sat down in my wheelchair and held my arms aloft as if I was a gymnast at the Olympics, landing successfully after doing some impressive somersaults.

This was an open-air event. As we were so early, we had to wait outside the makeshift venue for the gates to open.

It was June, still light and quite warm. I was wheeled over to the shade, and they lay on the ground to bask in the sun. I stayed in my chair looking at the makeshift venue, in this picturesque setting, with a big smile on my face, thinking, 'I'm at a gig!'

We were let in and sat about fifty yards to the left of the entrance, some way back from the stage. The wheelchair was quite difficult to push, even though the ground was hard and the grass was fairly short.

My companions lay down again on the ground, eyes closed, a plastic cup of beer resting on the ground beside them, and relaxed in the basking sun.

I sat bolt upright next to them in my wheelchair, one hand holding a plastic cup of not-beer, the other resting on the arm of the chair. I stared into the distance, feeling self-conscious again. I was convinced the few strangers that were there, were looking at me thinking "should he be here?"

After we'd been there for a while, the venue started filling up and the support acts started playing. The Zutons were the headline act and would be on in about two hours. We sat around in the warm, fading sunlight, just chatting, with the music playing in the background.

I was loving it just being around people again.

As this was a concert in a field there were Portaloos. There probably were disabled Portaloos but I wasn't yet accustomed to needing disabled facilities, so I just assumed I should use the same facilities as everybody else.

I would usually transfer from the wheelchair to the toilet via the turner. The turner wasn't here however. I had been provided with a plastic reusable bottle.

Having to go to the toilet was something I'd been trying to avoid. It had been playing on my mind since I found out I'd be able to come. I was hoping that if I barely drank, I wouldn't need to go to the toilet and I could put it off until I was back at the Haywood. I wouldn't have the humiliation of having to ask to be taken to the loo.

Unfortunately, my plan didn't work. The warm weather wasn't something I'd considered.

Drinking was unavoidable.

Laura pushed me over to the Portaloos and there was a small queue. We joined the back giving me time to worry and panic about how I was going to do this.

I caught glimpses of the inside while others took their turn and there was barely enough room for a person to stand in front of the toilet.

We got to the front of the queue, and it was my turn. Sure enough I couldn't fit all the way in to shut the door behind me so Laura stood guard. With minimal privacy I proceeded to do what was needed and then had to hand the now fairly full bottle to my girlfriend to pour down the toilet as I couldn't reach.

I was mortified. I really didn't belong here. I stared at the floor in embarrassment. I didn't want to look into anybody's eyes, as I imagined the whole venue staring at me.

Some of my friends with whom I saw The Zutons in Preston were at this gig. I had in my mind that this was going to be a big reunion. They'd be excited to see me.

It wasn't and they weren't.

In fact they were so unimpressed to see me that one of them decided to pour some of his beer over my head.

I didn't see it coming and didn't attempt to move out of the way. I didn't quite know what to do. My reaction in the past would have been to do exactly the same to him.

Those days were gone.

I was in a wheelchair; I couldn't reach his head. He was standing to the side and slightly behind me and I couldn't twist to see him and I couldn't move the chair.

I didn't want to be somebody people thought they couldn't have a laugh with. I tried to think how I could react. I tried to laugh it off, but it was clearly forced.

He realised his mistake and said he was sorry. An apology wasn't what I wanted. I wanted to be the guy who could take brutal revenge while laughing loudly.

The Zutons came on and everybody began dancing along to the music. The noise increased. I was struggling to make out what people were saying. I was watching people's mouths, trying to lip-read.

I had to shout to be heard. The louder I spoke, the fewer words I could say before I had to swallow.

I wasn't enjoying this.

The daylight made way for dusk and it became cooler. After the embarrassment of the Portaloo, I didn't drink anymore, hoping I could hold off until I got back.

I wanted to show everyone I was having a good time, and wondered how. I'd look like an idiot if I danced around in my chair. I couldn't sing along because I couldn't speak as fast as the song required - plus nobody near me would be too happy.

The view wasn't great from where we were as we'd parked up right next to the entrance. Now I saw that there was a raised viewing platform, closer to the stage, to give wheelchair users a great view.

Disability access was something that hadn't entered my mind; I'd never had to think about it before. I didn't see myself as disabled. I didn't want to be considered disabled.

Laura and I moved to the platform for the remainder of the gig. We couldn't talk because of the volume, so I just sat there and watched, thinking, 'Why am I here? She would be having so much more fun if I'd stayed in the hospital'.

The nurses welcomed me back with great enthusiasm. They were all so excited about my adventure that I couldn't bring myself to disappoint them. I told them what they wanted to hear; I knew this had taken some organisation.

"It was great to get out," I said. "I can't believe I've just been to a concert."

In truth I didn't enjoy it much and was relieved to be back. I felt completely out of place there. I was shattered, even though it wasn't that late, and just wanted to go to bed. I looked forward to tomorrow where I could be on my own.

People would enjoy things so much more if I wasn't there. They'd be able to go anywhere and not be restricted by wheelchair access.

# *Chapter 16 - Baby Food, Anyone For Tennis and Pottery Painting*

### An Idiot Doing Idiotic Things

I was driving through Stafford on my way home. The traffic was at a standstill, which back then usually meant there'd been an accident on the M6, and traffic had been diverted through the town.

Nowadays it happens if the day ends in a Y.

I was negotiating a roundabout and the traffic was temporarily moving freely, albeit slowly.

An almost car-sized gap had opened between me and the car in front. In the lane to my right was a blue Maestro with a body kit and loud exhaust. The owner had added even more weight, so the top speed was now probably even slower than my Nissan.

He wanted to come into my lane. He didn't indicate, he just started coming across like it was his divine right. I should have let him in, but I sped up to close the gap, all the while looking to the right and staring at the young driver.

*THUD*

My car came to a sudden halt. I looked forward and the front of my car was buried in a Peugeot's boot.

As I was getting out of the car, I glanced to my right and looked at the Maestro driver, who was smiling and waving his hand from side to side with his fingers curled.

I apologised profusely to the victim of my idiocy. He said it was fine as there was no damage to his car.

Unfortunately, there was no damage to mine either. God, I hated that Nissan.

## Back in Reality

It was around this time I was able to join the other patients at mealtime. Well, some of the time…

I was moved onto a diet of pureed food. You might call it baby food - basically anything that could be whipped into a paste. If there was nothing on the menu to satisfy this criterion, I would have to go back to being spoon-fed yoghurt.

Gaynor confirmed there was a meal that had been pureed for me and, as she was serving lunch that day, she took me up to the dining hall.

We went through the double doors and she asked me where I wanted to sit. I had no idea, I didn't know anyone. You might recall that I'd spoken to Pete, but I think it's safe to assume I hadn't made a good impression.

A guy called Malcolm said, "He can sit here." Gaynor took me over and sat me at the table with Malcolm, Geoff and Pete.

My baby food was brought over along with a tablespoon, and I tucked in. The first few times I attempted to stick the spoon in my mouth, I missed and jabbed myself in the face.

True to form, my intention tremor spotted I was holding the spoon, and saw its opportunity to shake. The pureed food was quite loose, so if the spoon hit an immovable object - like my face – I would flinch dramatically, pull my head back as if I was recoiling from a bee's nest, and the food would drop from the spoon onto my tee-shirt, where it blended with the dribble stains that were already there. My tee-shirts looked like a Jackson Pollock painting.

I had food caked around my mouth, I was wearing a bib, I had short hair, a perfectly round head and I needed someone to wipe my arse. Stick me in a highchair and you've got a twenty-five-year-old baby.

I was befriended by Malcolm, Pete and Geoff. They were very funny - Malcolm in particular. They seemed to know everybody, or everybody seemed to know them, or everybody was forced to know of Malcolm because he would be at the centre of any banter that was being thrown around the room. He was at the centre of it because he had normally started it.

When we were in the lounge, everybody would talk to the people on their table. Conversation was usually at a low volume, and then Malcolm would suddenly raise his voice to involve someone at a neighbouring table.

"Not like Margaret, eh Margaret?" Margaret would then join the conversation, and soon it would spread to the rest of the room. He was a genius at pulling people together.

The rehab unit was split into three, and I was in room two. Pete, Malcolm and Geoff were in room three.

There was an extremely nice guy in my room. Sadly, he was terminally ill and largely bed ridden. I only saw him out of bed a couple of times as he had to wait some time for a specially adapted wheelchair that he could self-propel with his one functioning hand. Unfortunately, he was soon too weak to use it and became a permanent fixture in the bed.

He was an incredible person. He was stuck in bed all day without a television or any form of entertainment. I can't imagine the boredom he faced and the negative thoughts that must have rattled around his head.

He was always pleased to chat and I never heard him refer to his situation - in fact I still don't know what was wrong with him. I didn't like to ask.

In the bed diagonally opposite mine was an Italian man whose wife was English. His wife was fluent in Italian and all their conversation was in that language. I wondered if he'd been equally fluent in English before his injury.

The human brain is a vastly complicated and baffling thing. Brain injury can cause people to speak in different accents or experience complete personality transformations.

In the Haywood was a woman who could now only say "Be able". Her inflection, though, was so accurate that she could convey considerable meaning, as though she was speaking full sentences.

"Do you want a cup of tea, Linda?"
"Be able."
"I can't remember, do you take sugar?"
"Be able."
"Thought so. Here you are."

The nurses would encourage her to stop being lazy and use proper words and, towards the end of her stay, I heard a few additions to her vocabulary. I often wonder if she recovered all those other lost words.

On the occasions that I was relegated to getting spoon-fed yoghurt by my bed, I'd finish it like a good little boy, remove my bib and be pushed by the nurse to the dining room. I was keen to be part of the group.

Then, after a couple of weeks, Malcolm had gone.

He'd been transferred to a care home in Manchester as he had no family, was in a wheelchair, and was incapable of looking after himself.

This was completely out of the blue to me. I don't know if Pete or Geoff were aware of it, they were in the same room as him, so they may well have been.

Unfortunately, he hadn't had a lasting effect on the atmosphere of the dining room. Everyone returned to chatting amongst themselves in their cliques.

```
16/6/08 Dietician

Discussed with Tom re having breakfast, snacks of
yoghurts and trying a supplement of fortyjuice - also
discussed starting to reduce overnight feed.


17.6.08

Tom has lost 4lb in weight. Thus, need to ensure Tom
has 2 Fortyjuice daily hopefully Tom will drink 2
during the day but if not could you please make sure
he has 1 when you visit.
```
Thanks Sue

```
30/6/08

Seen by dietician due to weight loss. Please could
you bring him more desserts/yoghurts in, so he can
have one when you visit in the evening.
```
Thanks Sue

## Anyone For Tennis?

Now I'd nailed step transfers[16] and the physios had told me "If step transfers were an Olympic sport, you, sir, would have won Gold."[17] They wanted to try me at tennis… I thought this was very ambitious and was going to be a pain to organise. "Really?" I said.

"But there isn't a court nearby so we'd need to get transport. The courts need booking. Not to mention I'm in a whee…" The penny dropped.

---

[16] My words.
[17] They didn't say this.

"Ooooh you mean play tennis on the Nintendo Wii? Oh yeah, that does seem doable."

The Nintendo Wii was a relatively new invention at the time and was the first console to use motion sensors, so if you swung your arm like you were holding a tennis racquet, the character you were playing on the screen would do the same.

The Wii was set up in the dining room where there was lots of room, a physio bed was brought in and put about two metres from the television. It was lowered so that I could sit with my feet on the floor. I was perched on the edge of the physio bed, so there was no backrest. I swayed like a tree in the wind.

I couldn't find my centre of gravity.

A physio sat beside me and put her arm around my waist to steady me, but still leaving my arms free. I prepared for a long rally, culminating in a delicately hit ball over the net.

The game is set up with me to serve first. The ball is tossed up, I reach my arm up and hurl it forwards.

I miss.

I thought I'd got my timing right, but the ball was already bouncing on the floor when I tried to hit it. The ferocity with which I flung my arm forward meant that I practically fell off the physio bed. My arm didn't move independently from my body.

The physio moves directly behind me and wraps both her arms around my waist. I'm instructed to reach for the ball with less ferocity and try to move my arm independently from my body.

Second serve.

I put so little force behind my motion this time that the racket barely moves. I miss again.

15-0.

Clearly power isn't the way forward, so I'll concentrate on connecting with the ball. I just need to get it over the net. The ball is tossed up.

Got it!

I fail to get it over the net. I fail to get it more than a few feet in front of me.

Another second serve.

Success.

I hit the ball with enough power to get it over the net. Hah! Bet my opponent wasn't expecting that! I can see the panic on his face, beads of sw…

Oh he's returned it.

It turns out he was expecting it, but the fool doesn't notice that I'm not very mobile and hits the ball straight back at me. I forget the 'more accuracy, less power' rule and swing with such ferocity that the physio has to call a colleague to get her shoulders back in their sockets.

I miss the ball and it's 30 - 0.

Right, I've got the knack for this now; I'm confident I can win the next point.

My serve sails over the net. It's straight at my opponent though, and he returns it with ease. This time he's spotted my lack of mobility and returned to another part of the court.

40 - 0.

I hit the net with my first and second serve and the game goes to my opponent.

Maybe I would be better returning serve.
Nah.
That proves to be even harder.
This is the easiest setting. If the ball was any slower it wouldn't be moving. By the time I've motioned to hit it and the shrieks of pain from the physio have finished, the ball is on the ground beside me.

The next ball isn't served straight at me. My opponent has found my kryptonite - making me move - and he's going to exploit it at every opportunity.

For the next point I do the unthinkable: my foolish opponent hits the ball straight at me and I return it.

It's gone to a different part of the court. He's in trouble. Beads of sweat are dripping from his forehead. At full stretch he barely reaches the ball.

He unsportingly plays the kryptonite card again and returned the ball out of my reach.

We stick at it for a bit longer to try and work on my coordination, timing and balance. We admit defeat when I fling my arm at the ball and the controller flies out of my grasp. Fortunately, there's a loop on the controller that wraps around my wrist, so the TV screen survives.

```
3.7.08 Physio:-
Today Tom used the slideboard to transfer onto the
single plinth with the assistance of two people.
While sitting on the edge of the plinth Tom played
tennis & bowling.
He also stood up with the assistance of 2 while
playing. Transferred back into the wheelchair. Good
session
                                                   Sarah
```

We tried the Nintendo Wii once more and even tried it standing up. Bowling didn't require any leg movement, and standing meant I could swing my arm without the arm of the chair getting in the way. And I was consistently getting the ball to the skittles, which barely moved.

I tried harder, but if I put any ferocity into the motion my body would lurch forwards.

We didn't try the Nintendo Wii again. The physios said if Wii Sports was in the Olympics I'd get the wooden spoon.[18]

## Pottery Painting

On a Wednesday, Bridget would come in with several different pieces of unpainted pottery for us to decorate. She would set up in the lounge and patients could attend if they wished, pick a piece of pottery and, over the following weeks, paint their own colour.

---

[18] They didn't say this either.

I think this was mainly for fun and general socialising, but it also tested various skills like coordination (placing the paintbrush on the pottery where you intended), dexterity (staying within the lines) and the heaviness or lightness of touch required.

Some people didn't seem to have coordination or dexterity problems and were very good at painting. Some would colour a flower realistically with a green stem and leaves and the petals in a different colour. Some would paint it multicoloured, not intending it to be at all realistic.

Not surprisingly, these were the people who tended to paint several pieces during their stay. They were very competent and finished a piece quite quickly and eagerly started another.

I assume these were people who enjoyed painting before, and their ability was unaffected. Maybe they hadn't done something like this before and realised they were quite good, and it was enjoyable.

Then there were people who were 'okay' but there was potential to improve with practice, and they found it enjoyable.

Then there were people who were rubbish. However, they'd improve with practice, and that was motivation enough to proceed.

I haven't included myself in these categories, because I was so bad, I deserve a category on my own. My attempt looked like it had been done by blind dog.[19]

---

[19] Actually, that probably gives the impression it was slightly better than it was.

When Bridget (or Breedge as she preferred to be known) and her pots came in, I'd spend the time on the laptop or have a nap. I knew I wasn't going to be able to do it, so I didn't have any intention of trying. In fact, it had barely occurred to me I could give it a go. I assumed because of my physical issues I wouldn't be expected to take part.

I didn't really know anybody, which I saw as a good reason not to attend. Breedge reasoned I wouldn't know anybody if I just stayed here and watched films.

"But I'll be no good at it."

"How do you know if you haven't tried?"

She'd got me. I couldn't really argue with that.

"Fair point" I said.

I was certain this would be a disaster, but I agreed to give it a go.

I wasn't very adept at this sort of thing before, I was fairly sure I would be even worse now. I've always been of the opinion that you don't do something unless you've got some talent for it. I didn't have much talent so I didn't try most things.

Breedge was coming from the angle that it doesn't matter if you're good, it's a chance to join in with the rest of the group.

She took me to the dining room, I chose the piece of pottery I thought was the easiest to paint, and I set about attempting to hold the paintbrush.

A horse would have had more success at holding the paintbrush. I'd prepare my right hand as if it were holding a pen, I would then place the brush in the correct position in my right hand via my left hand. My hand would shake wildly like a squirming cat trying to free itself from your grip.

Then I'd drop the paint brush.

Breedge would pick up the paint brush and hand it back to me, I'd receive it with my left hand and place it into my right like a pen again, this time holding it higher up the neck.

So now I'd tried it as Breedge suggested. And I was right.

'See,' I thought. 'I absolutely did know I'd be rubbish. Egg on *your* face'

I didn't have much control of the paint brush as I was holding it high up the neck. I tried my trick of tensing my body and jamming my left foot into the floor. It worked. Kinda.

I was able to control it better, but the blind dog was still doing the painting.

Breedge walked around the room offering each person encouragement.

"Good, well done" I'm sure she was fighting the urge to laugh.

I decided not to try painting again.

# *Chapter 17 – Swimming - Wait, What…Really? It's Grandad and Food Adventures*

Physiotherapy 11/7/08

Today we did bed work with Tom -> working on "switching" on abdominals + bottom muscles.

We also motioned feet to make them "accept" weight through the floor.

We then went straight into stepping practice and did x2 walks. 1 in the small gym + then in the large gym. Tom managed to walk the length of the gym with assist of x2 either side providing support + prompts. He particularly needed help to weight bear over right leg but overall he managed very well. His legs became tired so we finished there. His step transfer was nice today!

Claire G(physio)

Physiotherapy sessions largely concentrated on walking now. They were far less challenging than they were while my abilities were being assessed. Then, I'd work up a sweat just standing up or walking a couple of meters while the physios guided my lifeless body. We'd try all sorts of different things to see if they helped.

Now we'd tried almost everything and failed. I felt I'd plateaued, that I'd tried for Everest and barely reached base camp.

I began turning the physios away when they came to collect me; "I'm too tired" I'd say. I preferred lying on my bed or watching films.

It wasn't a very taxing existence.

I'd had the goal of going to the Zutons concert and worked hard at nailing step transfers. Since then, there'd been nothing to aim for; I was finding it hard to get motivated.

```
29|7|08

Physiotherapy

We did a hydrotherapy session today.  Tom's pelvis
is very stiff so we concentrated on motioning this –
with the buoyancy and warmth of the pool.

Tom was supported with floats around head + neck,
legs + feet.

He tolerated work very well.

                                            Claire G
```

I didn't know there was a swimming pool at the Haywood so when the physios asked if I wanted to use the pool tomorrow, my initial reaction was,

"Really? We're going to go to a swimming baths?"

"No, we'll use the hydrotherapy pool upstairs."

"Oh, yeah, okay."

I think they were expecting a more enthusiastic response.

I wanted to make sure their expectations matched my lack of ability.

"I'll be no good at it."

"How do you know if you haven't tried?" they asked.

'Why do people keep saying that?' I thought.

They explained that we would largely be doing our usual physio session, but with the added benefit that it would allow them to do exercises that weren't possible in the gym. The water would aid my ability to walk and balance by offering additional support.

My pessimism gave way to some optimism. I was going to have a change of scenery and a break in the monotony of the usual session.

I now had a new goal. I was going to stand unaided, walk unaided. Water was all that I'd needed all this time!

This was a step up from the last goal of a step transfer, not to mention delusional.

I asked Mum to bring some swimming shorts, goggles, nose clip and an aqualung from home. I was going to the swimming baths!

The hydro pool was upstairs in the physiotherapy ward. The changing room was divided into eight areas with a physio bed and curtains that could be drawn around it.

The heat hit me as soon as I entered. It was like a sauna. There was the unmistakable smell of chlorine that you normally get in swimming baths, but the temperature change was far more extreme. You could smell the heat. It was stifling.

The one clear lens on my glasses steamed up, rendering me temporarily blind.

I got changed and was wheeled through another set of double doors to the hydro pool. The heat stepped up a notch and the smell of chlorine grew even stronger.

I'd removed my glasses, so I was seeing two versions of everything I looked at, which made me wonder how I ever thought this was normal.

The pool was much larger than any hydro pools I'd seen. Granted, I'd not seen many, but you catch glimpses into football clubs' facilities on television, and theirs is only about ten metres long. This one was slightly smaller than your local swimming baths. You could swim lengths in this.

There was the customary shower nearby to encourage bathers to rinse off anything that could infect other people. A physio took the shower head off the wall and hosed me down as best she could without getting the wheelchair wet. I was then wheeled to the edge of the pool where I would transfer from the wheelchair into the chair lift that would swing me over the water and submerge me.

Successfully launched, we tried a stand. The buoyancy of the water made absolutely no difference. It was no easier to keep myself vertical. As soon as the physios let go, I started to topple - again falling mostly to the right.

I'd love to try this again. Now I understand my right leg doesn't reach the floor unless I extend it, and back then I had no sense of balance at all. I think I could stay upright for at least a few seconds now.

I lay on my back with a number of sausage-shaped floats looped around my arms and one more under my head. A physio pulled me into the centre with another walking alongside.

I can't remember exactly what the next exercise was, but I know it required me first to roll onto my side. With all the floats I was as buoyant as a cruise liner. I flailed about like a beetle trying to get back onto its feet. I hadn't got the muscles to roll, and the water wasn't offering the solid surface of a plinth. I tried sticking my arm out as if grabbing for an object. I tried pulling on an imaginary rope and hoped the momentum would roll me onto my side. Unsurprisingly this didn't work. Ok, on to plan B…

I flailed about with my legs, hoping they would create some momentum. Unsurprisingly this didn't work either.

I didn't get as far as the actual exercise.

After an hour's session I got back into the chair lift and transferred back into my wheelchair.

This was an unmitigated failure as far as I was concerned. The physios thought differently, and I had a weekly session in the hydro pool for several weeks.

I think they then agreed with my assessment.

## It's Grandad

Mum, Dad, my uncle and his partner came to see me outside of visiting hours.

It wasn't unusual to see my uncle and Kaz as, even though they live about three hours away, they had been to see me several times. They even came when I was in the ICU, when I wasn't at my most entertaining.

This didn't feel like a social visit though.

Their mood seemed to be sombre and Dad said, "Shall we go to the conservatory?"

That rang the alarm bells, I knew something was up. We went into the conservatory, closed the doors and sat around the table.

"It's Grandad" Dad said.

I feared the worst. "He hasn't died?"

Dad nodded and I broke down, sobbing quietly to myself.

I'd only seen him once since I'd been in hospital. I wasn't really in a state for visitors in the early days.

This was sixteen years ago, and I still miss him. Everybody in the family does. He was the patriarch of the family. He is still regularly spoken about, quotes of his are thrown in conversation between family like an in-joke.

I don't really remember anything else about this visit, but I think that's probably because it was quite short. I was taken back to my bed and they left.

My mind wandered. This was completely out of the blue. He was eighty-seven but it seemed like he could have gone on forever. He'd always been incredibly fit. His health had worsened over the last few years, but I never considered him ill or frail.

My dad had found him sitting in his armchair with the television on, a cup of coffee and some chocolate caramels next to him. Earlier that day he'd driven to meet some pals at a cafe. He'd died peacefully in his sleep.

That's a comforting thought, now as I write this, but I didn't know any of this at the time, so I found little consolation. Instead I felt guilty.

I'd barely seen him in the last year. It was little comfort that I'd not had the opportunity, and now I felt guilty that I'd rarely gone to see him while I was able to - he only lived thirty-minutes' drive away.

I felt alone. I couldn't talk to anyone, actually, scratch that, I could have if I wanted to. There were several people to talk to.

Sue came to see me the following day, saying she was sorry to hear about my Grandad. I've no doubt she was offering me a shoulder to cry on.

"Thank you, it was unexpected. Have you seen Cloverfield?"

It probably wasn't the reaction she expected, but she accepted my obvious deflection of her sympathy.

## Food Adventures

```
7.-8-08 OT

Hello!    Tom   has   been   to   supper   club   this
afternoon/evening! Made beans on toast - pretty well
except for setting fire to the grill and shoving his
hand on the hot grill pan! Aiming to make home made
burgers within the next 4 weeks (if we manage not to
burn the place down in the meantime!)

N.B No injuries apparent!

                                                  Alice
```

Supper club was intended to get patients back in the habit of preparing a meal. This was something I'd been very adept at. I was as good as a Michelin-starred chef.

Honest. On occasion I've even been known to use the oven instead of the Microwave. The peak of my culinary skills was when I made tea at home, putting the chips and mini pizzas in the oven - at different temperatures for different lengths of time!

Go on admit it, your opinion of me just grew a little, didn't it?

This was like rocket-science to me, and it was my first and final attempt as biting into a still-frozen chip almost broke a tooth.

I was still on a puréed diet and couldn't eat normal food yet, but I was going to progress to a normal diet at some point, so this would be good practice.

Alice asked me to try supper club.

"I'll be no good at it"

"How do you know if you haven't tried?" came the response.

'Fair point' I thought with a feeling of déjà vu. 'Looks like I'll have to prove *you* wrong as well.'

I knew that if I didn't agree to try, Alice would have asked again, and again, and again, until I decided it would be easier to relent.

"OK! I'LL GO!"

She asked me what I'd like to make.

"Burgers".

It would have been more achievable to say "I fancy a bowl of Rice Krispies". Although it would be touch-and-go as to whether I could manage that.

As it was my first time attending, Alice said we'd work towards the goal of homemade burgers, but first she suggested beans on toast.

I wasn't going to be able to eat my inedible food anyway, so it made no difference to me what I 'made'.

I was going to cook the beans after I'd put the toast on and, well, the toast part didn't go well. I didn't get as far as the beans.

I like toast.

My recent toast-cooking experience was limited to using a toaster. This kitchen had a cooker with a grill.

I'd made toast under a grill at my parents' house when I was younger. I was pretty confident with my extensive toast-making experience; I could make the toast on whatever apparatus they had.

I put the bread under the grill and turned it on. After a couple of minutes, the bread was turning golden and, as I'm probably the best toast-maker in the world, I reached in to turn it. Without thinking, I used my right hand.

I'd forgotten that my right arm waves around like Rimmer's salute in *Red Dwarf*. It brushed against the glowing orange grill. Another incident to remind me I'm not a righty any more.

I had warned Alice I'd be no good at cooking and her relentless nagging led me to third-degree burns.

I hope she struggles to sleep at night.

```
15/8/08 Physio

Tom's been to breakfast club this morning where he
made his own breakfast. Straight after Tom went upto
the gym where we worked on his bed exercises, also
rolling on to his front to stretch his back.   Tom
also walked approx 20 metres with 2 physio's.  Good
session today Tom, well done.
```
Vicky.

Breakfast club had the same intention as supper club, but you would do the washing up afterwards.

This was fortunate, as I was probably the best in the world at washing up. They were playing to my strengths.

Again, I wasn't going to be able to eat what I prepared, but as I love my toast far more than cereal, I opted to return to the scene of the crime and make toast again.

"Are you sure?" Alice asked, sliding the box of Rice Krispies across the work surface.

"Yes thanks." I slid the Rice Krispies back towards her.

A call was made to the burns unit and they were told to expect my arrival.

Even though I wasn't going to be able to eat the toast, I asked for Marmite.

I carefully put the bread under the grill with my left hand and under the watchful gaze of Alice. She wasn't reassured enough to trust me to flip the bread and then retrieve it.

It smelled divine.

I attempted to put the knife into the tub of margarine with my left hand. It was a strange, un-natural feeling; I was clearly using the wrong hand. It took me several attempts to get enough. I was trying to get just enough and not take a big lump.

Try as I might, I couldn't spread it evenly. More marge was on some parts of the toast than others and I had tried to get to the edges, but unintentionally fallen short. I tried to rectify it, but the knife would fall off the toast and spread margarine on the plate.

I tried my right hand instead, I knew this was shaky and inaccurate, but would at least feel natural. My arm waved around and eventually plunged the knife into the marge.

I scooped too much Marge onto the knife and left it there. I didn't think I'd be able to scrape the right amount off the knife, it would probably be all or nothing. The toast was unevenly spread and I didn't go anywhere near the edges as I knew I'd get more on the plate than the toast.

I joined the other two patients for breakfast. They both had toast and I probably added to the drool stains on my tee-shirt while I enviously looked on.

We did the washing up afterwards.

This is what I was here for. I was going to show them my world-class washing-up skills.

One person did the washing-up, another dried, and the other put away. I headed straight for the sink and left the other two to decide their roles.

The sink was at wheelchair height, so I didn't have to reach up.

As always, I showed no patience. I turned on the tap to fill up the sink in world-record time. Water hit the bottom and ricocheted onto my glasses. I turned the tap down a bit, ran it until it was hot enough, and inserted the plug.

Five seconds later, the sink was already almost full. Slightly panicky from the speed the water was leaving the tap, I reached with my right hand to turn the tap off. I turned it, but it needed another revolution. As I repositioned my hand for another turn, I returned the tap to full blast. The water edged closer to the top. With some urgency now, I tried again.

The same happened. Water started pouring onto the floor. In a blind panic I switched hands and finally turned the tap off.

I looked at Alice sheepishly, expecting her to tell me off.

"Nice one," she said ironically.

I decided against pointing out that this wouldn't have happened if she hadn't pestered me to come. It was all her fault.

# *Chapter 18 - Clunk, Click Every Trip, Conversion and No More Physio*

From the end of August, I was allowed to spend weekends at home.

Home was a twenty-minute drive and the amount of travelling needed meant a one-day excursion wasn't worth it. I would go home on a Friday and return on Sunday.

This – like The Zutons gig – was going to be a return to my previous life. I was extremely excited and as far as I was concerned, everything would be the same as it was.

Dad arrived to pick me up and he helped me do a step transfer into the car. There was no point using a turner, as we'd have to do it this way at home anyway, and as I mentioned earlier, my step transfers were now Olympic standard.

I was excited about seeing my cats. Archie and Molly were great characters, but Molly was my favourite. Whenever I sat to read or watch TV, she'd always come for a cuddle.

I imagined it being like one of those YouTube videos, where the person has returned from years spent away with the army, and their dog is ecstatic to see them.

We bypassed the front door, as there was quite a big step up. I hadn't thought about how I would get in, but this avoidance of the usual entrance woke me up to the dose of reality I was about to endure. There was a back door in the garage, but there was a similar two-inch step into the kitchen. Fortunately, we had a small conservatory, which only had a small lip to get over.

This already didn't feel like the home I remembered. I had been pushed past the front and back doors and brought through the 'special Tom entrance'.

We had a smallish living room, well stuffed with furniture. Molly, my big black cat, was lying on the sofa. As I rolled towards her saying "MOLLY!", she scarpered into the kitchen. I followed her re-assuring her, "it's ok".

As I got closer she fled outside via the conservatory.

On the wall underneath the living room window is a large sofa. Its size meant that I couldn't get to the door leading to the hall. It only granted access to the stairs, which I knew I couldn't use anyway, but it was something else that was now out of bounds to me.

Obstacles came from unforeseen areas. A thin rug in the kitchen made it hard to move the wheelchair. The carpet in the living room presented more friction than the smooth floors of the hospital.

Laura had a good eye for décor, and I liked the way the house was decorated, but it was furnished with practicality for an able-bodied person.

To get from the kitchen to the living room you had to steer around a small Ikea sofa, which meant angling the wheelchair. It would then scrape against the door frame.

The small sofa was pushed up against the large one. People had to climb over the large sofa to get to the hall door.

A small camp bed was laid out in the living room.

I'd been going home for the weekend for a couple of weeks and I was in the kitchen, chatting.

I removed my glasses to give them a wipe, but my hand started squirming until I dropped them on the floor. I leaned forward to pick them up, which is something I'd never done before so I didn't think of putting the brakes on. I reached down and the redistribution of weight caused the wheelchair to roll forwards. I fell out of the chair onto the quarry tiled floor. It was only a short distance, but I didn't put my hands out to reduce the impact, so my knees broke my fall.

It didn't hurt much, but my right leg felt a little strange. I assumed I was okay and shimmied into a sitting position and, with my girlfriend's help, got back into my wheelchair.

We went into the living room and watched a film. I wasn't in pain, but I didn't feel comfortable. I couldn't find the words to explain it, I couldn't say what was causing discomfort, I just felt a difference in my right leg. I'd fallen on my knees, so it seemed logical for the discomfort to be there. I squeezed my knee but there was no pain. Yet something felt *wrong*.

I couldn't concentrate on the film. I couldn't find the words to explain myself; words that made sense in my head didn't make sense when I said them out loud. After a few minutes I told Laura something wasn't right. I wasn't sure what it was; it couldn't be serious as I'd got up off the floor. I was trying not to get to upset as I'd just had a bit of a fall. I became increasingly worried that I'd jeopardised my discharge.

I asked her to phone my parents as I wanted their advice as to whether I should go to hospital to get it checked.

I kept repeating, "I can't have done any damage. I got up." But I was becoming more and more anxious and agitated.

They came over and had to calm me down. In the short time they'd taken to come over I'd let my imagination run wild. I was distraught and panicking about the damage I'd done and had convinced myself I wasn't going to be eligible for discharge now. I was crying and annoyed I hadn't put my brakes on. They reassured me that it wasn't too bad as I wasn't in pain and a fall like I had isn't likely to cause a break. But to be safe we'd go to A & E.

The four of us got to the hospital. The step transfer in and out of the car was uncomfortable and I didn't fully extend my right leg, but it was taking some weight, which again suggested it wasn't serious.

My Dad asked me where the pain was, and I still wasn't sure. I felt pressure to give a satisfactory answer. I couldn't just say "dunno" and shrug my shoulders, so again I said, "my knee".

I was seen fairly quickly. I lay on a bed in a side room and told a doctor I'd hurt my knee.

I didn't say "I *think* it's my knee" because I didn't want to have to try explaining why I didn't know. At no point did I tell him that I was currently an inpatient at the Haywood, or that I had diminished feeling on my right side.

My knee was x-rayed, and it showed no damage.

I was assigned a bed and told to wait for a doctor to come and see me. The four of us waited ...and waited. After eight hours spent in the hospital and in the early hours of the morning, we spoke to a nurse who told us we were still on the list. She put the X-rays onto a CD for me and I discharged myself.

Back at the Haywood, the physiotherapists would come to my bed, every day to collect me. I was finding it quite painful to use the leg, and on several occasions would choose to stay in bed.

I tried to explain the pain and its location, but again all I could come up with was the knee. I wasn't trying to be misleading, but without being able to locate the pain and considering the fall that caused it, I tried to self-diagnose. I should have just been honest and said I don't know. Hopefully that would have prompted them to investigate the whole leg. I drastically delayed its diagnosis.

11.09.08 Physio

We have been keeping an eye on Toms knee this week + have been popping some ice on it. I have done various tests and it doesn't seem that there is any ligament damage + I know nothing was picked up on xray. We tried a stand between two which Tom managed OK. Not too much pain but when we tried to step it was far too painful so we did sitting balance work instead.

Claire H

Physio (Monday)

Tom's knee seems slightly better today, we managed 3 stands with assistance of 2. He was able to put some weight through his knee & straighten it. He stood for about 1 minute each time. We also did some bed ex's for his abdominals + bottom muscles.

Claire E

Physio 19|09|08

Physio session in gym.

Knee exercises (see sheet) to be done over the weekend. 2x10 in the morning on the bed and 2x10 at night on the bed.

We also worked on abdominal muscle strength.

Claire G

24|9|08 Physio

We did lots of abdominal work today in lying and strengthening work for his R knee. His R hip was particularly sore today so we are going to request the Doctors review his hip.

Claire G

The doctor review wasn't until the following day. Rather than wait and probably send me for another X-ray anyway, one of the physiotherapists hoped to skip this step and have a look at me first. I lay on my back on the bed, and straightened both of my legs so that my toes were pointing at the ceiling.

There was a noticeable issue straight away. My right foot wasn't pointing up at the ceiling. It was turned forty-five degrees. I tried to return my foot to the centre so my toes were pointing at the ceiling, but I couldn't. It wasn't causing me pain to try, but it was now clear, my knee wasn't the issue.

I had another X-ray. This time my attempt at a self-diagnosis was ignored, and the hip was X-rayed this time. This revealed that I'd broken the neck of the femur. I was whisked off immediately for an emergency operation at North Staffs. Again.

The repair involved literally screwing the neck of the femur back in place. I have a three-inch scar on my right hip. It's very strong, but I have reduced lateral movement on that side.

The day after the operation, two physios came to my bed to help me to stand. I was extremely apprehensive; this seemed very early considering my leg wasn't even properly attached yesterday. I shared my professional medical opinion, the one that had identified this as a knee issue.

Really?" I questioned "Already?"

"Your leg has been re-attached to your hip with a screw. It will be as strong as it used to be. We need to confirm there's no pain when you put weight on it."

I decided to trust the medical advice and stood up, putting all of my weight on my left leg. They assured me my right would take the weight. I shifted my balance bit by bit, transferring more each time my leg didn't crumble. It held. There seemed to be no difference from before the break.

I was in this hospital for four days and I realised why I didn't mind my stay at the Haywood. In the rehab unit there was a sense of freedom, there were a few rooms you could go in, there were always activities going on, games to play, all of the staff knew my name without having to check the clipboard at the end of my bed.

At North Staffs I was confined to my bed, and I didn't know anyone. It was incredibly boring. I had a book with me, but I found it hard to hold, my right hand in particular would constantly wobble and my eye struggled to focus unless what it was focussing on was still.

I still had visits every day to look forward to. I would clock-watch, waiting for my visitors. After looking forward to their arrival, I would spend the entire visiting period watching the clock, getting more and more depressed as the time for them to leave got closer and closer.

# Conversion

22|8|08

```
Hello! Tom showered this am - did well again.  Also
worked on feeding at lunchtime - did really well
again - used normal cutlery and didn't drop much.
Just to let you know - turner + commode ordered for
home, so local store in your area should be getting
in touch with you to arrange delivery.
```

Alice

Alice came to see me after my leg break, but prior to it being identified.

I assured her that it was a fall as a result of my stupidity and that the environment was fine for me to go home to.

I would have said that if I was returning to a World War I bunker, and Alice knew it. She wanted me to start thinking about my discharge and preparing my home environment to cater for my needs.

I hadn't thought about the future for a while; any dose of reality had upset me to be honest - trying to play the guitar, The Zutons concert, Grandad dying.

I was quite content at The Haywood, my existence was easy and completely stress-free. There were certain disadvantages, but it catered for all my needs. Life would never be this simple again.

I explained that I lived in a house and the only bathroom was upstairs. The shower was a head mounted on the wall connected to the taps. I'd have to step over the side of the bath to use it.

The front door is about two inches up from the driveway. There is a backdoor into the kitchen although it has a similar step-up issue.

However, there is a large garage attached to the house. It's about thirty feet long and could easily be converted into a living space. No building work would be required as the building already existed.

Alice said she would contact Social Services to see about getting the garage converted into living quarters. She was happy for me to go home while a permanent solution is being readied.

Then the problems started.

Alice phoned the Social Services and was told they wouldn't look at doing the conversion because they needed to assess me in the already converted environment to see what needs are required to be catered for.

There was a major problem with this ridiculous rule. The Haywood couldn't discharge me until they were happy I was going back to an environment that catered for my needs.

Alice made them aware of the situation and let them know I couldn't go home until the conversion that they were refusing to do was completed.

Neither side would budge. I was in limbo.

My Dad and my brothers volunteered to do the conversion. In true Jeremy Clarkson fashion, they thought 'how hard can it be?'

Alice asked Social Services if they would at least fund the conversion.

They wouldn't.

They said as they're not doing the work, they wouldn't fund it.

I simply don't know what happened here, maybe there were some crossed wires. This was something Alice had organised hundreds of times. She was great fun but also seemed brilliant at her job, she was a real ally and somebody who would have done her utmost to help me.

The problem as far as I'm concerned was Social Services, though when I've used them since they've been great. Admittedly, they've only project-managed modifications, but things have gone incredibly smoothly. I think whoever was running things at this time is to blame.

Fortunately, my family took on the financial burden as well as the physical exertion.

I'm not sure what the original idea was but it quickly evolved into a plan for a bedroom, a separate room for a bathroom and a small garage at the end.

Adam worked next-door to the office of a bathroom company. They donated a brand-new sink and toilet, along with the materials and expertise to create a wet room.

Dad, Daniel and Adam would probably rather wrestle a crocodile than try a build like this again. They spent every weekend from October to December working on this conversion.

It now had a wall separating the living quarters from a small garage (which has since been converted into a utility room, a modification overseen by The Social Services). Thanks to the generosity of the bathroom company, I now had a fully accessible bathroom. The company went out of business shortly afterwards. I hope I wasn't a contributory factor, but they'll always have my sincere gratitude. The bathroom was just going to consist of a commode and turner without their help.

## No More Physio

```
Physiotherapy 27|8|08
Worked in standing with a high plinth in front -> Tom
practiced finding his own standing balance.  This was
better today and he only needed minimal help.

We walked Tom with a zimmer frame today -> Just to
give it a go but it didn't work for Tom.  We walked
then between 2.  His walking was then much better.
Much more upright - controlled steps so we will
definitely not try the frame again.
```

Claire G

Walking with a Zimmer frame was a disaster. It's designed to improve confidence and independence, and reduce the risk of falls and injuries. It became evident that somebody was always going to have to be present when I used it, which kind of defeated the point.

The aim is to put some weight through your arms and hold the hand grips. You stand between the back two of the four feet, so that your weight is coming from above.

The frame was very light and incredibly easy to tip. If I positioned myself as they told me, I fell backwards.

Standing further back put too much weight on the frame. Lifting it to move forward involved leaning back, and then my only contact with the ground was my legs. It was very much a case of 'what goes up, must come down'. I had a couple of seconds before I had to put the frame back on the ground, so that my weight could slam down on it.

On the odd occasion, the Zimmer frame would land where I intended, but most of the time it would land exactly where it already was. I would lift it again, fighting not to tip to the side or need intervention to stop me from falling backwards.

We admitted defeat and switched it for a rollator. This had two wheels at the front. meaning I could just roll it forwards instead of having to lift it.

It was as light as the Zimmer. It would start rolling away from me while I was standing. If a physio didn't put a foot in front to stop it, I'd have looked like Mr Bean trying to hold onto it as it moved further and further away.

```
Physio 28.08

Worked on Tom's sensation and perception in his feet,
with a good stretch to his calf muscles.  Then worked
on sit to stand push off + controlling movement.
Further work in standing - work on transferring his
weight onto each leg + lifting alternate hands off
plinth.    Did  very  well  -  only  requiring  min
assistance.  We finished by walking between 2 15m -
improved control + positioning of feet.
```
Claire G

```
1.9.08 Physio:-

This afternoon helped Tom onto a peanut ball (a bit
like a gym ball Tom shall show you!) to work on his
balance and to give his hips a good stretch.  Bouncing
up and down.  Also holding a small ball with both
hands.
```
Sarah

We scrapped the walking aids and tried sitting on a gym ball - A large inflatable balance ball. I would sit on that with my feet planted on the floor, and my torso leaning forwards at forty-five degrees.

I was sitting unsupported but dared not move.

```
4/9/08 Physio

You have done a really good job with Tom's right foot
as it is now far more supple.  We worked on Tom's
feet to start with.  Tom did some core stability
exercises on the bed.  We worked on high sitting
balance, worked on sit-to-stand with minimal use of
hands.  Standing balance training.  Walked approx 4m
between 2 with good control.  Tom remains very wobbly
trying to put on his shoes.
```
Claire H

I'd been doing physiotherapy since February. It was now September, and I was still only doing sit to stands, and walking four metres with the help of two physios.

All attempts at using walking aids had failed; swimming had failed; playing Wii Tennis had failed. Basically, I had failed at it all.

They certainly couldn't be accused of not trying everything possible, so when the head physio joined my monthly goal-planning meeting, I knew it wouldn't be good news.

I liked her, I think I got on well with her, but to be honest, I'm not positive. I didn't have as much fun with her as the other physios. If she was in a session, it seemed more serious. But that's how it should be I suppose. The boss isn't there to make friends.

I'd been having monthly goal-planning meetings all the time I'd been at the Haywood. The goals were things that would show clear improvement in my condition. Initially it was goals like talking, moving onto a pureed diet, beating Brian at chess.[20]

The goals moved onto things like practising step transfers, attending the Zutons concert or staying at home on Friday and Saturday night.

This was great motivation to keep moving forward and was making me feel I was constantly achieving something. Now I'd run out of goals. There wasn't anything else achievable and my place at the Haywood was being held only because my home environment wasn't suitable yet.

I was informed that I wasn't going to be able to have physiotherapy as regularly as I had been. I wasn't showing enough progress to carry on getting treated regularly on the NHS in place of somebody who did show more progress.

I didn't argue. This wasn't out of the blue, my home environment would be ready soon, meaning I was going to be discharged.

My NHS treatment was going to end soon anyway, so it didn't really matter how this end came about. The physiotherapist said it was important to continue with regular physiotherapy and she recommended I see Lynne Fletcher[21] at Manchester Neurotherapy Centre. This would have to be at my expense, but she felt it important to continue with regular physiotherapy. To remind you,

---

[20] This was never a goal, there was no chance Brian would let me win.
21 As a patient this time, and not because of my supermodel looks.

Lynne was the magician who'd previously had me walking with minimal assistance.

I had an assessment with Lynne. Two physiotherapists from the Haywood came with me - Claire G and Claire E.

I was at MNC for an hour and a half, and a lot of this time was taken up with Lynne concentrating on my right leg – doing her Mr Miyagi magic.

After my hip was repaired, a measurement was taken of both legs to determine the difference in length. I can't remember the actual figure, but it was unrealistically large.

Claire shared this figure and Lynne looked like she'd been told the sky is yellow with pink polka dots.

"Is that implied or actual?"

"Actual."

"Hmm," Lynne muttered quietly. "I'm not convinced."

As she had done at the Haywood, Lynne began to manipulate my leg. This time it took much longer. It was quite uncomfortable but bearable.

She measured the difference and it had significantly reduced.

To finish I did a walk of a few metres with just Lynne. It was anything but perfect - I still wasn't confident on the right leg – but Lynne could achieve more on her own than three conventional physios. Lynne was as strong as an ox, but more than anything it was down to her advanced Bobath skills. She knew how to hold and support me.

# *Chapter 19 - Buh Bye, Social Services? That's Ironic and Dignity Has Left the Building*

By the end of November the conversion wasn't finished but it was taking shape nicely. Alice, a psychologist and a social worker took me on an excursion to see if what was being done was appropriate.

We were all blown away!

I was wheeled down the driveway and went past the front door through the opened garage door.

The garage was now much smaller and held the washing machine, dryer, fridge freezer and a few odds and sods. We had quite a bit of stuff stored in the garage beforehand, but it was nowhere near enough to warrant the size of garage we'd had.

My new bedroom was at a higher level and a ramp was in place. Inside, the floor had been boarded and was ready for laminate tiles. The door into the kitchen was now level with the bedroom floor, so I could get to the rest of the house.

Two new walls had been erected, creating the wet room. The walls were boarded ready for a plasterer to complete the job.

The conversion wouldn't be ready by the time I was discharged, but the social worker was happy for me to use a camping bed in the living room while work was completed.

I was discharged on the fourth of December but the last day I spent in hospital would be Friday twenty eighth November, as I only had to show my face and sign a form.

A few days before I left, I was sent to another part of the hospital to have the tube connected to my stomach removed. It had barely been used over the last few months and had just been something to constantly irritate me by snagging on my clothes.

The end of the year was approaching, and they were a little short-staffed as people were using their holiday before their quota was reset. A temporary nurse took me over to a different part of the hospital. She was Eastern European. Her English was very good, but I was convinced she would find me unintelligible, so I said as little as possible. We travelled in silence.

After a fairly long walk we arrived in what appeared to be a completely different hospital. It felt like we'd gone through a portal and come out several years in the past.

I was a little nervous as I wasn't sure how they were going to remove this tube, I said to the nurse I needed to go to the loo.

I was still requiring assistance from the nurse at this time for the immediate aftercare duties.

A few weeks previously a nurse called Julie was unsure why I wasn't wiping my own arse and encouraged me to try it myself.

"You're going home soon, we won't be there to do it for you."

"Fair point" I thought.

Without thinking[22] I used my right hand – it takes more than third-degree burns to convince this idiot to use his left. Holding toilet paper and not being able to see it means I don't know if I've dropped it.

You can see where this is going.

I wiped but the toilet paper wasn't in my hand. I was familiar with Julie though and able to deflect the embarrassing situation by holding my hand up and saying, "That's why".

I'd never met this nurse and I'd convinced myself there would be a language barrier. It was going to be incredibly embarrassing to ask her to wipe my arse. So I didn't. My usual attitude of avoiding the tricky situation and hoping for the best was in full flow again.

I knew the pitfalls this time, I knew that the way I held the toilet paper last time was the issue and I knew that I had to concentrate hard on feeling if the toilet paper had fallen from my grip again; after all I did have a little sensation in my hand.

My hand vanished from my view, firmly holding the toilet paper. I moved my hand very slowly so the movement of air didn't dislodge it. 'Done it!' I thought, 'textbook!'.

---

[22] As usual.

It wasn't textbook. The toilet paper had dropped, and my short-lived optimism was about to become longer lasting embarrassment.

'Oh shit!' I thought.

I looked at my hand. Yep.

The embarrassment was going to be unbearable. I hoped if I took long enough, she'd knock on the door and ask if I'm okay. I'd find it a bit easier to broach the subject if she initiated the conversation.

It didn't seem like she was going to though, so I sat on the loo building up the courage to call out.

I didn't know her name. "Excuse me?" I said to the door softly, half-hoping she wouldn't hear.

"Hello?" She replied

"Can you come in?"

I hoped we shared a common sign language and held up my hand. I'd escaped the indignity of needing my arse wiped, but it wasn't much of a victory. I silently watched her uncomplainingly cleaning up my rancid hand.

I was starting to consider myself left-handed.

We went into a room that seemed like a small theatre for less essential procedures.

I got up onto the bed, manoeuvred onto my side and... I can't remember exactly how the tube was removed. It didn't hurt and it took about thirty seconds. The hole closed by itself, not even needing a stitch. Like my tracheostomy, it left a visible scar that over the years has completely gone.

I said my goodbyes over a few days as people were around at different times depending on the shift they were working.

I went to get my guitar off Brian, and he told me I could only have it if I beat him at chess.

'Bit harsh' I thought 'I've never beat… oh, hang on, he's going to let me win'.

We played the final game and he was shockingly bad. I mean so bad it was almost like he was trying to lose. Still, a bet is a bet and I left with my guitar.

On the day of my discharge, the only nurse I saw regularly was Lee. The place was incredibly quiet with almost no people around.

Lee said "It's bittersweet at Christmas. You're hoping people get better so they can go home, but most do at Christmas and the place is dead."

I sympathised, shook his hand, said my thanks and went home…

Putting my time at the Haywood in writing makes my experience seem much harder than it actually was.

In many ways I actually enjoyed it. I was living in the now. I was just experiencing things as they happened and didn't think about how my future was going to be affected. Sure, I had my down days, but that was as a result of how I was feeling at that moment.

I was part of a community with people I considered friends. Everybody was in the same situation. I had at least one visit every day, and on weekends I had two. I didn't feel out of place as I have done repeatedly since.

The nurses were fantastic. They really looked after me, and I don't think I was unique in that, they cared for all of us that way.

Most importantly there was no pressure, I was in an environment that shielded me from the stress of real life.

It was a rocky start at the Haywood and not being able to speak made things very difficult, but as time went on I hope looking after me wasn't too much of a chore.

My return home was fairly low key as there was a mad rush to try and get this conversion ready for Christmas, so we could wake up in the new bedroom on Christmas morning.

It would be a stark contrast from the previous Christmas which I spent in the Q.E. on the high dependency ward.

Dad came to collect me on his own as I had a guitar, wheelchair and ten months of accumulated things to bring home. Space in the car was at a premium.

I was feeling on top of the world.

This is what I'd been hoping and asking for since I told Dad "I want to go home". He said it wasn't possible, the little fibber. All it took was for he and my brothers to convert the garage.

Simple.

I was going back to a very different existence. I was going back to a world where I had to make the effort to talk to other people, physios weren't going to be telling me exactly what I needed to hear, I wouldn't have cheery nurses to make me drinks. I wouldn't be able to sit around watching films and then roll to the dining hall where my meals were waiting for me.

I needed to get back to earning money, which I didn't realise at this point wasn't going to be possible. I hadn't considered the practicalities of what I used to do.

Previously I had to talk on the phone constantly. I had to write several emails a day. I had to operate a computer with speed, I had constant deadlines to achieve in order to get paid. I had to drive to see people. I needed to be presentable.

This time I took notice of the front door as I was wheeled past it into the garage.

I wasn't feeling on top of the world anymore. I was feeling extremely sorry for myself and couldn't help thinking I'll never use that front door again. An unusual thing to focus on, but I was feeling emotional and picking up on everything that I could be negative about.

I was pushed up the ramp into the bedroom where Adam and Daniel were waiting. There was now plaster on the walls and ceiling.

It looked phenomenal.

There were dust sheets throughout, so I was limited to just this bit of the conversion. I looked over the rest of the room. Archie, one of my cats, was asleep on a stepladder at the end of the room.

I called him, but he didn't stir. He was out of my reach for now, but he'd have his opportunity to react as Molly had later.

I wheeled myself into the kitchen and rubbed against the door frame as I was trying to rush and hadn't lined up the wheelchair correctly.

I felt awful, they had spent all this time and effort on it and the moment I'm back I mark the door frame. It wasn't the end of the world; the walls had only just been plastered so the room needed to be decorated.

I wasn't used to having to line up the wheelchair to get through doors. There was always so much room in the hospital; you could fit four or five people side-by-side in the area outside my ward. There'd been lots of room around my bed. More often than not I'd been pushed around. When I did self-propel, I could rush around without thinking about bumping into stuff.

Now I was home, that had to change. I had to think about how I got from A to B, if I didn't I would bump into things and scrape walls, door frames and radiators.

The floors in the hospital were smooth and wheelchair-friendly. Here, the thin rug in the kitchen slowed my progress to the conservatory door. From here I could only peer in. The conservatory was tiny. In addition to its usual furniture, the sofa from the living room was propped against a wall. The camp bed I'd be sleeping on was in its place in the living room.

I turned around and self-propelled into the living room. It was easier now that the second sofa had been removed, but the carpet was harder to roll on.

I wheeled into the middle of the living room, turned to face the telly and realised these were the only rooms I could get to.

People were watching me with smiles on their faces, waiting to see my elation. I felt I had to paint a smile on my face to show the excitement I thought was expected of me. I wanted to say "Is this it?" But that would have seemed ungrateful, a lot of effort was being put in so that I could return home.

I'd had completely false expectations of what my homecoming would be. Now I felt that, outside of my family and girlfriend, I didn't matter to anyone. I had said my goodbyes to everybody at the Haywood, but I was expecting people to be a little more upset or sad.

They had done their job brilliantly. They'd made my time as pleasant as possible, but they say goodbye to people every week.

My leaving was their goal and they'd achieved it.

## Social Services? That's Ironic

Care had been arranged with Social Services to get me up in the morning, help me with washing and dressing, and make me breakfast.

A key safe was screwed into the wall and a set of house keys were put inside it.

The first morning that a carer came into the house to get me up, she saw the turner that she would use to get me into the wheelchair and said, "I've never seen one of these before".

"Oh really? There were about ten of them at the Haywood," I replied.

I would say she was in her sixties and about seven stone wringing wet. I explained that I would stand on the turner, rest my knees against the knee pads and pull myself up with the handlebars. She should stand opposite me, anchoring the turner, and turn the handlebars so that I'd be in position to sit on the wheelchair.

The carer didn't make the turn in a continuous motion; she jerked it round and I became unstable, swaying and trying to keep hold of the handlebars. The carer lost her balance and fell backwards onto the television table, banging the TV against the wall. I fell sideways over a pouffe, and hit my head on the wall. I dragged myself back to the bed and pulled myself up. The carer had nothing to say about the incident.

The next morning, she was accompanied by her boss, who told me that she wasn't happy with the situation her carer had to come into. She wanted the pouffe removed from the living room before she would be happy for the carer to keep coming to the house.

I found this completely unfair. The room had previously passed inspection by a care worker. Not only that, but the accident had occurred because of a carer who wasn't trained to use a common item of care equipment.

I tried to voice these facts, but I stuttered and struggled to get my words out. Talking was – and to a lesser extent, still is – a labour-intensive process. I need to plan my words, and this takes time. A sentence would sound fine in my head, but once I started to say it out loud, I'd realise I needed to word it differently. I'd try and think of another way to say it, but by now they'd started replying. Now I'd have to respond to what they'd just said.

I'd stutter and struggle to get my words out, but they'd interrupt again while I was assembling my next sentence.

I gave up. I couldn't fight my corner, and I was aware I needed these people's help.

We moved the pouffe into the already cramped conservatory.

At least they were now happy with my environment…

## Dignity Has Left the Building

I presumed coming home meant that I would get some dignity back and I would be able to start doing things for myself, but I'd underestimated how much the nurses did for me, and the convenience of the environment I was in.

The first time I prepared a drink was an eye-opener. My kitchen wasn't built for people in a wheelchair, and the work surface was quite high. My shoulders were up around my ears as I reached up. I grabbed a fairly full bottle of Coke from the fridge and struggled to lift it. Now I needed to tip it into the glass. I used my right hand to hold the base of the bottle, but my arm was shaking and wobbling.

I tipped the bottle and some of it poured onto the work surface.

In a panic I moved the bottle over the glass, but my arms were tired. I let the bottle rest on the glass, but it tipped over, and more poured onto the work surface.

After I'd fallen out of the chair again, and hit my head on the toilet bowl, I had to promise to wear a pendant with a panic button. A press on that would connect me to somebody, so I was always able to get help.

I felt like I was in a care home. I just needed the stairlift and walk in bath to complete the set.

I couldn't go anywhere. I couldn't get out of the house, and I couldn't self-propel if I was outside - The uneven, rough terrain was too hard to navigate.

Then there was the toilet. My nemesis. The subject of so many humiliating situations in the past.

I'd brought back a plastic reusable bottle from the Haywood. Most of the time I was on my own, so my dignity would remain intact, when using it.

However, my first night home, *wasn't* one of these occasions. We decided to watch a film.

True to form, I hadn't thought about needing to go to the loo, and how I would deal with it when the moment arrived. I started to notice it was going to be necessary, and didn't drink any more, hoping to put it off for as long as possible.

I realised that was stupid.

I was going to have to ask for my girlfriend's help at some point; I was just delaying the inevitable.

"I need to go to the loo, could you grab the bottle?" I'm sure I turned bright red when I asked.

She jumped straight to action - as with the nurses in hospital - it wasn't an issue. I now felt embarrassed for feeling embarrassed.

The bottle was handed to me, and she left the room to give me some privacy. I called her back when I was finished and handed her a full bottle to dispose of. I'm sure my bright red complexion returned. The toilet in the wet room hadn't been installed yet, so she had to go upstairs to dispose of it.

When the downstairs loo was available, she still insisted on doing it this way, to save me the hassle of transferring and getting onto the toilet.

A big deal was never made of this, and it became normal... for me.

I didn't consider that she hadn't signed up for this. She was now having to be my carer after she'd done a full day's work.

There are times where a toilet is required. I had the commode that Alice had ordered for me, but I draw the line at shitting in a bucket.[23]

On these occasions I would call my parents.

They are only round the corner, about a minute's drive away and they would come round as quickly as possible and take me back to their house.

---

[23] My motto is: "will shit in boxes, but not buckets."

Fortunately, I had become quite adept at using my left hand at this time. I didn't want a repeat of the incident with the Eastern European nurse.[24]

When the downstairs loo had been installed, I still called my parents (if I was home alone), because I couldn't transfer on my own at this time.

If my Dad came round, I would stand with him in front of me, put my hands on his shoulders and transfer round to the toilet. If Mum came round, I would transfer using the turner.

I'd been able to go to the toilet without help from anybody else for over two decades.

Going to the toilet is something everybody does but it's not something we talk about. I don't like having to announce to people that I need to go to the toilet. I feel like the whole room stops and waits for me to return, debating how long I've been gone and discussing what I'm doing. I half expect people to clap and cheer when I come back.

Walking with an aid hadn't improved since my Haywood days either. Mum and Dad would come down most days and aid me with walking with the rollator. I still needed to be watched very closely and constantly prevented from tipping to the right.

I would walk the length of the bedroom. I was sure this was never going to be as quick and as safe a mode of transport as the wheelchair, but I listened to the advice of

---

[24] Not that my parents had an Eastern European nurse available.

"practise" and didn't take my usual defeatist attitude of "I'm no good at it, so I won't try."[25]

I wasn't anywhere near being able to walk independently. You couldn't even call it walking. I was alone until Laura came home from work. Then I'd be a burden. I couldn't play my guitar, my cats hated me, I had to wear jewellery around my neck with a big red panic button on it, and the Social Services seemed hell-bent on trashing my house.

There was only one thing for it, the answer to my self-loathing.

Eat, eat and eat some more.

I was back up to my pre-surgery weight, as I'd taken advantage of the three meals a day on offer at the Haywood. I'd had some practice at making my own food in hospital. Granted, you might say that didn't go well, but I had the proper tools here (toaster), and a non-faulty grill.[26]

I was confident(ish). Not particularly hungry, but particularly bored.

I got into the kitchen and remembered the high work surfaces.

I had a genius thought, give me a food puzzle and I'm suddenly Albert Einstein! I decided to have a bowl of cereal, take the components into the bedroom and put it on my desk, which is lower.

---

[25] I eventually did stop as I was no good at it. See, point proved! A defeatist attitude saves time.

[26] It definitely was faulty. I am the best in the world at toast making remember. You're only as good as your tools.

I took the deconstructed breakfast into the bedroom, forgot about my right hand and poured the milk into the bowl, drenching the floor and splashing the keyboard.

I spent ages cleaning that up, which did kill some time, but my urge to eat still needed attention.

I continued thinking like Einstein. I brought my portable table from the living room into the kitchen and gave my world-class toast-making skills a go.

I put the margarine and Marmite out, fumbled around trying to grab the bread from the packet and retrieved a couple of slices, putting them in the toaster.

After a couple of minutes, warm, golden toast popped up.

'See Alice, safe as houses.' I thought, as I reached for the toaster with a metal knife in hand. Not really… it had a plastic handle.

I had the same butter-spreading issues I'd experienced at the Haywood. Parts weren't covered, some of it had too much, and the plate was now covered.

For the pièce de resistance, I added Marmite. Or I tried to.

It had taken me so long to partially spread the butter, it wasn't melting. I spread the Marmite on top.

I put the plate on my lap, wheeled to my desk, and ate cold, badly spread toast.

## Chapter 20 - My Disability Has Its Perks, The Speech Therapy Journey Continues and Jolty Fingers

One advantage of taking so long to finally get around to writing this book is that I can tell you about some of the advantages to my current situation.

I couldn't see the wood for the trees at the time. It's 2024 now though. I'm not twenty-five and new to this.

I'm forty-one.

Wiser.

Still an idiot…

In 2006 when I bought my house, the majority of houses had gas central heating. So - as you would expect from an idiot doing idiotic things - I bought a house with Economy Seven electric heating. There were storage heaters mounted on walls throughout the property.

As always, I didn't think about the need to change this outdated heating solution and just assumed I would be in a position to change it at some point in the future.

As it happens, I was right.

2009 started with a letter from Xtrawarm. They would install central heating in my home. I can't remember if Xtrawarm was a company or part of a government initiative to keep us vulnerable folk warm.

Either way, they would remove my old economy seven heating, take the storage heaters off the walls, and install a combi boiler with five radiators. It was about £2500 of free modifications made to the house.

Now that I was back home, I received a benefit called Disability Living Allowance. The four-weekly payments consisted of a care component and a mobility component. Any motor dealerships taking part in the Motability scheme would provide us with a brand-new car, and my mobility payment would go direct to them.

I booked an appointment with the head of Motability at my local Ford dealer, and after a short discussion agreed on a brand-new Ford Focus. The car was the exact value of my mobility payment, which went straight to Ford. It was simple and hassle-free. A yearly service was included, and I could choose a new model every three years.

Compared to my Nissan Almera, it was total luxury. Although, a shopping trolley would have been an improvement over that abomination.

Making toast and having cereal hadn't gone too well, so my obvious solution was chocolate. Tins of the stuff! Celebrations, Roses, Quality Street and Heroes.

What can I say? I like chocolate, a lot. And I was bored, a lot.

I had access to mirrors now, and unfortunately they weren't distorting my reflection like a hall of mirrors. I really had ballooned. I needed to get to the gym, but money was a little tight. I couldn't justify committing to a regular payment.

It was time to learn of another benefit.

I was able to get exercise on prescription, and because I have a prescription fee exemption card, I wouldn't pay a penny.

I went to a participating gym several times with Adam. I would go on the stationary bike, where I would sit on a highbacked chair, get distracted by the TV and rotate my legs just enough to register as motion.

After this excellent gym session, I would celebrate by having some chocolate. My vigorous gym session had probably burned off a corner of a Heroes, so progress was being made...


I have a blue badge, which does not allow me to be in control of a vehicle[27].

It allows me to park in disabled bays, although it frequently appears that *not* having a badge affords one the same advantage.

I remember seeing a Facebook post some years back, of a woman sitting in her wheelchair behind her mobility van that she couldn't get in to, because somebody – without a badge - had parked right up to the edge of the neighbouring disabled bay.

Parking in a disabled bay was a choice for the able bodied, but a necessity for the disabled woman. Still, it saved someone thirty seconds of walking...

---

[27] The arresting police officer was puzzled that I thought it did.

Most importantly, I received two invitations through the post to the outpatient rehab ward at Cannock Chase Hospital and then Moor Green Rehabilitation Centre.

They both continued the rehabilitation process started at the Haywood. There were twenty or so patients attending each one – all as outpatients. They offered various group-based sessions like painting, woodwork, cognitive strategies, current affairs, Book Group and managing emotions. As well as more physio and speech therapy.

Speech had become a real issue since I'd left hospital. Even though I avoided it as much as I could while I was at the Haywood, there were always lots of people around, so there was still, some communication.

I was on my own a lot more now, which suited me fine, but when the opportunity to speak to people was there, I wasn't taking it, and my speech was suffering.

The Speech Therapy at Cannock largely mirrored the work I was still doing with Barbara Molteno.

The speech therapy at Moor Green seemed much more thorough than Cannock and every activity was with a group of people.

The managing emotions and cognitive strategies groups at Moor Green were exactly what I needed. These were smaller groups with around six other patients. We'd all discuss our issues, and, because I wasn't the only focus, I found I was more relaxed. Quite often somebody else would describe an issue, that I was experiencing also, meaning it could be discussed without me needing to talk.

An example that sticks out in my mind, is a discussion about phone calls. Somebody raised the subject of their anxiety about talking on the phone.

'This could apply to me,' I thought, so I paid particular attention.

I wouldn't say my apprehension is anxiety; I just didn't want to subject other people to the stress of understanding me. I found it frustrating when they hadn't understood my ramblings and interpreted what I said incorrectly.

I didn't want to take the focus from this person's issue, so I just sat and listened. It was suggested that simply holding the phone to her ear might be triggering the negative feeling of making the call, so try setting the phone to hands-free. 'What a good idea' I thought.

I was holding the phone with my shaky, inaccurate right hand, and holding it to my left ear because my hearing is weaker on my right. This freed my left hand so that I could prod the keyboard of my computer to take notes.

I was frustrated before the phone call even started; it was no wonder I wanted to end the call as soon as possible.

Book Group and current affairs at Moor Green required members of the group to read to the others, and we would all discuss.

This exchange applied to nearly all the groups. There was camaraderie. I was becoming more confident as time went on, because more and more people, were becoming aware I had speech difficulty. It wasn't just thrust upon them.

I was a regular fixture at Moor Green for quite a few months, and I started to gain confidence and join in. People initiated conversations with me and didn't seem to regret their decision as I was rambling at them.

## The Speech Therapy Journey Continues

Barbara started regular house visits in January 2009. Once a week initially, but after a few months, we decided to change this to once a fortnight.

I'd email her several recordings a week of me reading a passage from a book, and she'd email back with advice. I found this form of therapy invaluable.

We worked on adding some intonation into my speech. I wasn't going to be able to alter the pitch much, but people would find my speech easier to follow, and more interesting, if I altered it just a small amount.

This nearly always required a fresh breath, giving Barbara an excuse to bang her breathing drum again.

When I took an intermittent breath, Barbara would metaphorically smack me across the knuckles and tell me to take the breath from my diaphragm.

I could do it if I concentrated, I think…

I still wasn't sure how you control your breath with your abdominal muscles, but she obviously wrapped me around the knuckles often enough, as breathing intermittently is a thing of the past now.

She was a keen singer and encouraged me to sing to myself around the house.

"I can't sing."

"Have you tried?" She'd ask.

"No".

"Well then, how do you know…"

"…if you haven't tried." I finished her sentence. I couldn't be bothered with this conversation again, so I belted out a song.

I proved my point. I couldn't sing. It sounded exactly the same as it does when I talk. The only indication I was singing a song, would be if I was singing a line of a song you recognised.

I would sing to myself for about ten minutes, but always in the newly converted bedroom, with the bedroom door shut. The neighbours might have heard me talking to myself and have me committed otherwise.

Daniel drove me to an appointment with an ENT at the Haywood. Barbara met us there. It was to try and identify what was causing my speech difficulties.

The doctor used a camera on the end of a bendy stick thingy (I think that's the medical term) and inserted it up my right nostril and then down my throat next to my vocal cords.

He said that my right vocal cord was constantly vibrating so fast that it looked still/static to the naked eye. He called Barbara over so that she could have a look.

A few months later I saw another ENT specialist at my own doctor's surgery. Mum took me, and the same process occurred, but this time the camera transmitted video back to a monitor that I could see. The right vocal cord was vibrating ridiculously quickly. It was so fast, it was like flicking through a deck of cards. One of those slow-motion cameras off a David Attenborough documentary would be needed to see it properly.

The specialist wrote a letter to my GP and sent a copy to me.

23 April 2009

Many thanks for referring this young man who I saw today. He has had a significantly stalling post-operative time following his left cerebellopontine angle haemangioblastoma excision.

He was seen in November 2008 by the ENT Department at North Staffs who felt hc had a left sided vocal cord palsy. His voice has become stronger since then and on examination he has some involuntary movements of his right vocal cord but both vocal cords move fully in there range of movements if not quite normally. There is no significant vocalis atrophy and his voice is strong.

Over all there is no requirement for ENT intervention at this moment and I hope that my findings are of use to the Speech and Language Therapist. If any further explanation is required I would happily pass the flexible nasoendoscope in the presence of the Speech and Language Therapists so that they can see for themselves the clinical findings. I am, however, very encouraged that we are continuing to see improvements in Thomas and I hope he continues to do well with time.

Best Wishes

Yours sincerely

R G M Hughes

Barbara also helped me with my writing. It's not something that had been looked at and with my performance in painting pieces of pottery, it was clearly something that needed attention.

She would bring exercise sheets with her some weeks. They had simple exercises, like an image of a basic shape such as a spiral, that I would try to replicate. Another example would be a picture that I would need to colour in, taking care to stay within the lines.

I struggled even to hold a pen. It was so thin that my hand would constantly squirm like a cat until I dropped it. Barbara fitted a grip to the Biro, which gave me a thicker surface to grab.

I could hold the pen now, so I had no excuse for my failures.

I was able to make shapes on the paper. They were legible, but they looked as though they'd been written by a three-year-old in the back of a moving car. To make them more legible, I'd tense my shoulder to steady my arm. I'd jam my left foot into the floor. These were effective techniques, but it would take so long to write just a few words. It was a solution that was too painful to implement for long.

Without this tactic my handwriting became large and messy. Often, I would run out of space on the page because my arm wasn't tired and hurting at the start of writing a word, but was by the time I finished.

I got ever so slightly better as time went on but the attempt at the spiral was only identifiable as a spiral because it was on the same page as the example, so it was clear that my attempt was supposed to copy this.

I had improved from a three-year-old at least.

My attempts now looked like those of a five-year-old.[28]

## Jolty Fingers

I needed to earn money. For financial reasons as well as my sanity and self-worth. I was sure I could still manage to do what I used to. All that was required was to sit at a computer. I was sure I could manage that, although I'd conveniently forgotten about what happened at the Haywood.

I proved that I couldn't physically manage it. My mind wasn't capable either – even though I was convinced it was.

At this point I hadn't done any research into earning money on benefits. I assumed that anything I earned would go on top of what my benefits gave me. That wasn't the case.

Back then I received Disability Living Allowance (DLA) and Incapacity Benefit, DLA wasn't means tested and what I received from it wouldn't be affected by anything else I earned. Incapacity Benefit was means tested. Work for more than sixteen hours a week or earn more than £167 and it would be stopped. Still, I'd be working and at this point I believed my output would be all that it had been before.

A previous client came to see me and gave me a job to set up a blog for him. I told him of an idea I'd had before I

---

[28] I hadn't stayed within the lines, something five-year-olds are congratulated for, but it's not good enough when I do it.

was in hospital that would use similar methods to what we'd worked on before, but it would need to be built from scratch. He agreed, although I think it might have been out of sympathy and with no expectation he would actually get a workable blog from it.

He had to come to me as I couldn't travel (previous meetings had been at his house). He'd seen with his own eyes this Gollum-like creature in a wheelchair, who couldn't speak clearly. I think he'd realised the reality long before I did. I think everybody realised the reality long before I did.

Operating a computer was a slow process, I was still knocking the mouse off the desk, I was still prodding the wrong keys on the keyboard. Nothing had got better, and I hadn't learnt any techniques to speed things up. It was taking much longer than I'd thought it would. Paying my mortgage relied on this and I was feeling under immense pressure and stressed to the point of tears because I was realising that I wasn't going to get this done in time.

This had been the only thing I was vaguely good at.

At the time I was hospitalised I was using technology that was becoming outdated. I was right on the cusp of getting left behind.

It was outdated now, and I had been left behind.

I was self-employed so if I didn't work, I wouldn't get any sick pay. I hadn't any critical illness cover on the mortgage.

I thought that a keyboard with bigger keys would solve my problem with pressing the wrong keys. I searched for "big letter keyboards" and came up with results for toddlers' "my first keyboard" and various toys.

I didn't think keyboards that moo at you were going to be a big help.[29]

After a bit more searching, I found what I was looking for. A keyboard with slightly larger keys. It looked like a Fisher Price toy. It was colour-coded. The numbers were blue, the arrow keys were red, the vowels were purple and the consonants were orange.

It made little difference.

I spent most of my time in the bedroom trying to get this job done. I was holding my neck in one position so I could see all of the screen with my one eye. My head slightly cocked to the right, I was tensing every muscle in my body, jamming my foot into the floor trying to force myself to be stable.

After a day of this I noticed that the index finger on my right hand was jolting. This would only happen after I woke up.

I noticed, when clenching my hand like a fist, upon release, my index finger would straighten slightly slower than the others and would jolt into the straightened

---

[29] Educational, yes, but I was twenty-five. I already knew a pig goes "moo".

position, as if it were a switch, that could only be in the on or off position. After a few days of this, my middle and fourth fingers became similarly affected. They were all jolting, loosening after a few clenches. A few days more, and the middle finger had become the biggest problem and I had to forcibly straighten it, when releasing my clenched fist.

There was never any pain, but it was concerning me.

I told Mum and Dad, and they got in touch with the Haywood. I was able to bypass the need to get a referral from a GP. The doctor suggested I have a steroid injection in each hand, so a needle was jabbed into the gap between my middle and fourth finger of my right hand.

The doctor asked me to slowly stretch my fingers and then move them slightly inwards and bend them like a bear claw.

He barked "SLOWLY!"

The same process was repeated with my left hand, and I realised why the doctor raised his voice earlier, I moved my fingers very slowly and it was quite uncomfortable. As was proved when I had the broken hip, there was a distinct lack of feeling in the right side.

# Chapter 21 – Counselling, Eyes and the Physiotherapy Journey Endeth

Counselling wasn't something I really wanted as talking had become my least favourite activity, but it was something I thought that somebody in my situation should do.

And maybe I just wanted to talk to somebody. Anger seemed to be my natural reaction to everything now. It tended to build up unless released, and apparently a problem shared is a problem halved.

I was angry about the lack of help I'd been getting from the state. I thought that I would have lots of help; any information required - like the benefits available to me - would be volunteered. But this didn't seem to be the case. It seemed that you had to ask the correct questions to the correct people. If you didn't ask, you didn't get.

It was frustrating. One is normally shown the ropes in a new job. Here, apart from not knowing the answers, I was expected to know all the questions.

I visited my GP who put me on the waiting list for counselling. And, for once, things happened fairly quickly.

My first meeting was with a psychiatrist[30] named, if I remember correctly, Sarah. Unlike my previous counsellor (the fat pigeon incident), she didn't close her eyes while she was talking. I found this encouraging.

I was asked general questions about what had happened to me, my daily routine, my general mood, my relationship, hobbies…

The important part of successful counselling is for the patient to be completely honest. Instead, I gave the answers I thought would convince her I didn't need a psychiatrist.

A short while later, a letter arrived offering me six weekly sessions.

I hadn't had counselling before, so my only frame of reference is TV shows like The Sopranos, and six sessions didn't seem enough even to scratch the surface.

I still wasn't very good at the whole talking thing, even though I felt I understood my speech issues a lot more now. But I wasn't used to talking so much and for so long. My jaw started to tire very quickly. I was sounding like Rocky Balboa and slurring my words.

These counselling sessions actually had a negative impact on me rather than a positive one. I didn't want to take part in any more of them, but felt I had to because I realised I wasn't giving them a chance. This pretty much summed up my attitude to most challenges.

---

30 …or possibly psychologist or psychoanalyst. I'm kind of unclear on the distinctions, though I know they're important.

The process was stressing me out, but I felt forced into attending.

Come September, Sarah told me that she was leaving to take another job, and that my case was being transferred to somebody else.

This happened to be with a different organisation, in a different building. I found my first meeting with David embarrassing. He had to rearrange the room so that I could get in.

He asked me if I wanted some water.

"No thanks."

Actually, I would have liked some, but I'd struggle to drink it unless it had a straw, which I was too embarrassed to ask for. He'd already had to rearrange the room; I didn't want to feel any more awkward.

As a newcomer, I was asked to complete a questionnaire. David read out the questions and I gave my answer using a scale of one to five, one being very poor and five being very good.

Typically, I answered all questions four or five, as if there wasn't a problem.

For the remainder of this hour, I gave David a summary of life over the past two years. I'm sure I only told him the bare minimum as I raced to the end of my sentence, eager to finish talking.

I liked David a lot. He was a very good listener. The counselling sessions became much more two-way and I felt encouraged to work through the pain of speaking for long periods.

During one session, he asked me what music I was into.

"Pink Floyd, Oasis... a lot from the sixties to today. Especially Indie."

"Are you familiar with Athlete?"

"Yes, *Tourist* is one of my favourite albums, why?"

"My son, Joel is their lead singer."

Athlete were a serious name at the time, so I was hugely impressed. And more impressed still when David invited me, along with my Dad (also a fan), to a concert in Birmingham.

It was a fantastic gig. The audience were committed fans, and Joel kept up a real two-way conversation with them between songs. It was a small venue – only about 300 people – and the whole tour had been planned to avoid the huge stadiums and return to Athlete's roots, playing intimate gigs for proper fans. It felt as though we were sharing a small room with our mates.

After a spectacular set and several encores, the band left the stage and the audience really got into its stride. Athlete's biggest hit was *Wires*, a song about the difficult birth of Joel's daughter. It was a moving moment when everyone began singing – and kept on singing:

"*I see it in your eyes, I see it in your eyes. You'll be all right.*"

Visibly moved, Joel returned to the stage, thanked everyone and played a final song, solo, just him and an acoustic guitar.

I count it among the best gigs I've ever been to; but there was more to come.

"Right, come and meet Joel," David said, and we set off to head backstage. This proved to be challenging, as we needed to negotiate a flight of stairs. David and Dad began the struggle, but this was Birmingham; two complete strangers immediately came to help. Together, they lifted the chair with me still in it, and we reached the bottom intact.

Backstage, we chatted at length with Joel. He was warm and welcoming. He said that David had told him about me, and he seemed genuinely interested in how I was doing. Like his, father, a thoroughly nice man.

## Eyes

While attending Moor Green rehabilitation clinic I met a woman who also suffered from double vision. She'd been given the temporary fix of masking tape over one lens. Then, one day, she came in with no tape and two apparently clear lenses.

"Didn't you have a frosted lens?" I asked.

"Yes, I've got a prism now, I can see normally using both eyes."

She took off her glasses and showed me. The left lens had a temporary film stuck to it. It had lots of tiny crosses, but was unnoticeable unless you knew to look for it. What appeared to be crosses was hundreds of tiny prisms that work together to reposition the image from one eye so that it coincides with the other.

I was familiar with this method; I'd previously had several consultations in which we'd tried to correct my double vision with prisms, but the disparity between my eyes was too much for them to fix.

"So was mine, but I had surgery to reduce the difference."

She gave me the name of the consultant - Mr Burden at Selly Oak Hospital. I made an appointment with him immediately.

I arrived at Selly Oak Hospital for my appointment and had an extensive eye examination. The optometrist outlined my options, firstly to surgically correct the double vision, but sometimes the brain loses the ability to overlay the left and right images. If that turned out to be the case, I could choose to have an opaque lens inserted into one eye, effectively blinding it. I'd then be able to wear normal glasses. The operation was reversible, so not as extreme as it sounds. I felt strangely reassured. I liked the thought of returning to my normal "look".

The eye examination began, and she mainly focussed on the eyes' ability to follow objects around the room without moving my head.

I couldn't see very far to my left, objects moved out of my field of vision quite quickly. She noticed that my right eye was misaligned; the left eye behaved as expected but the right eye was always looking in a slightly different direction.

My eyes were constantly darting around. They were never still. It took a second to re-focus on different objects, and I was constantly re-focusing as my eyes tried to drift upwards, as if on a conveyor belt, into the back of my head.

I was called in to see the doctor who did a few of the same tests to see the eyes' ability for himself.

"I understand you're keen on surgery?"

"I am, I don't like having a frosted lens, it makes me feel really self-conscious, but it depends how invasive the surgery is. I don't want another long stay in hospital."

He explained the issue with my eyes.

"There are six muscles (three per eye) that control the movement. Vertical, horizontal and tilting (when you move your head position). The muscle for tilting isn't firing."

He gave me a brief idea of the operation but didn't want to reveal too much until I see Mr Burden in six weeks, when he's returned from holiday.

'You're not Mr Burden?' I thought.

Mr Burden explained that I would require three operations, spanning over eighteen months, to reduce the distance between the two images I was seeing, concentrating on one area at a time - the tilt, the horizontal and the vertical. If all went well my eyes would see images that the brain could then merge into one.

He stressed this might not be the case though. He could fix things medically so that the difference between the two eyes was within the limits that prisms could correct, but the brain then needed to merge those images into one.

If the brain had lost this ability, then my hope of not needing a frosted lens could only be achieved by inserting an opaque lens into one eye.

He suggested we start with the correction of the eyes and review options after.

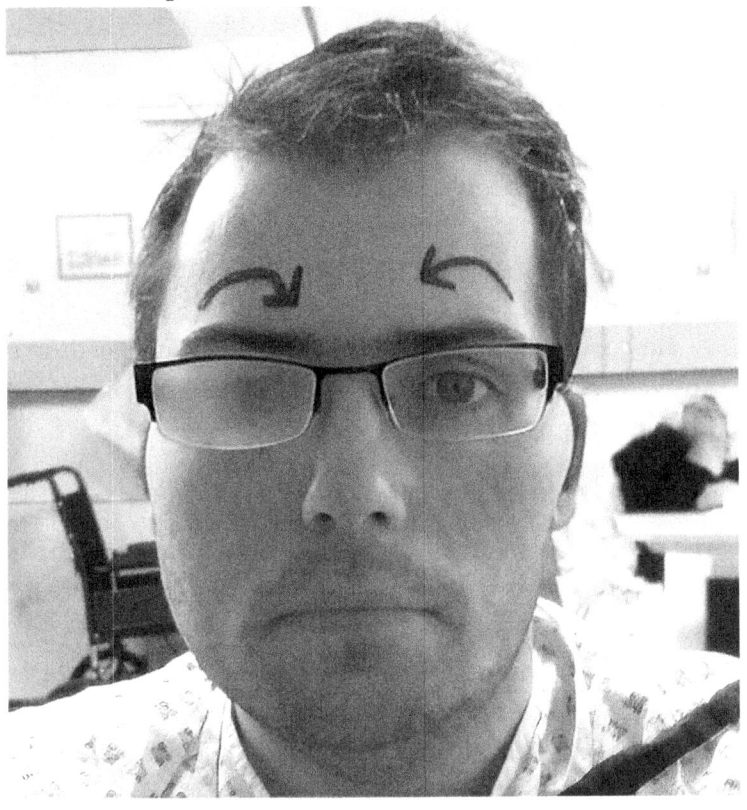

The operation to correct the tilt would take fifteen to thirty minutes. I would need to be at the hospital for eleven o'clock and, provided the anaesthetist was happy, I could go back home on the same day.

An incision would be made into the eyeball. The muscle responsible for the tilt would be tightened, like pulling on a piece of rope to reduce slack. They'd sew the incision with a couple of dissolvable stitches. My eye would be sore and red for a little while, but would recover quickly.

I was discharged a few hours after the operation and able to go home.

My eye recovered in a week or so, but I noticed a difference. When looking at a picture on my wall through my glasses, and then looking over the lens, the second image was no longer rotated. Moving my head closer, or further away still determined the position of the second image.

I attended a meeting several weeks later at Mr Burden's request. Mr Burden and his colleagues again stressed that eighteen months and three operations later, there was a chance I would still require the opaque lens solution.

I thought about it and decided to give it a go anyway. I knew it wasn't likely to be successful, but I would rather have attempted it rather than wondered "what if".

It was recommended I try wearing an eye patch to simulate only having vision in one eye. I might think it would be much the same as it is now, but I might rely on what I can see around the lens more than I realise.

I had visions of looking like Johnny Depp in *Pirates of the Caribbean* but instead I looked like Sloth in *The Goonies*.

It turned out I did rely on the peripheral vision of the right eye. I could see the profile of my nose and nothing beyond it. If something was happening on my right side, I couldn't see it.

I relied on my right eye more than I realised. I phoned Mr Burden's office the next day and cancelled further appointments.

## The Physiotherapy Journey Endeth

I continued receiving bi-weekly physio in Manchester for a couple of years. Lynne was extremely impressive and I felt I was in the best possible hands.

But as with physiotherapy at the Haywood, progress plateaued. I was doing the same exercises, and not particularly well. It seemed like an unnecessary hassle when I could just find something more local. Lynne was the best, but it felt like getting Pep Guardiola to coach a Sunday League team. I didn't need the best, I just needed to practise.

I parted ways with Lynne and turned to local therapists.

I spent the next seven years with all kinds of different physiotherapists. I used a mixture of NHS and private physios who would come to my house.

Around 2012, Social Services funded a few modifications to my house. One of them was to change the garage part of the conversion into a front entrance. A permanent ramp was attached[31], creating a nice long area for me to practise walking with assistance. When I'd

---

[31] See, they can be quite helpful, and no televisions were harmed.

walked into the house I'd turn into the kitchen. The memories of my broken hip still haunted me. The moment my feet touched the quarry tiles, I'd stiffen up. When I stuck a leg forward, my shoulders would go in the opposite direction. I was instantly nervous to walk on that surface.

Falling just a short distance from sitting had broken my hip, what would falling a longer distance from standing do?

I tried standing on a wobble cushion. I would stand on it with my arms extended in front of me like a zombie. The physio would hold my hands and I would… wobble.[32] I can't balance on my own two feet on a solid, flat surface, so you can imagine how this went.

Sitting on the wobble cushion was similarly unsuccessful. The damn' thing kept moving. The only way I could sit still was by pressing hard on the floor with my legs, and with my torso leaning over my left leg.

I had physiotherapy during rehab at Cannock and Moor Green. They tried me with Zimmer frame's, rollators, exercise balls and crutches.

I was as useless with the frame and rollator as I'd been on my previous attempts, and I found it similarly impossible to use the crutches. I couldn't place them where I intended on the floor, particularly on my right. I settled for wherever it landed and didn't try to correct its position; doing so would be equally inaccurate. I couldn't put my weight on it and swing through without the crutch collapsing.

---

[32] It wasn't just a clever name.

I tried walking with support from two physios. I wasn't holding their hands for support, so I found it hard to get the momentum to move a leg through without something for my right hand to pull on. I was all over the place, trying to balance on my own. I was stopped from falling to the ground several times.

I was finding it impossible to explain the problems I was having. I could explain in a way I could understand, but it didn't make sense when I tried to explain to others.

After numerous years, with many different physiotherapists all with different approaches. The advice from the Haywood of "practise, practise, practise," ringing through my ears. I felt I knew enough to do it on my own.

I knew what was working for me and what wasn't. I couldn't make people understand what would make my arm feel heavy and hurt. I couldn't explain what was making my hand feel tight, or my rib cage hurt. I couldn't explain that walking in a particular way was hurting my right leg, or my right knee.

My difficulty in communication was a stumbling block again. My solution was to cease physio.

# *Chapter 22 – Headway, All Clear and New Zealand*

I learned that I could attend Headway for two pounds a week. This was the charity I'd seen on a poster in the A & E ward in Stafford hospital. I didn't read it then; it was just a poster. Even though I was in hospital because I had a brain tumour, I still didn't consider it was relevant to me. I did have other things on my mind. Reading posters probably wasn't high on the agenda.

Headway is a charity set up to give help and support to people affected by brain injury. There was a community centre about fifteen minutes away. It was a chance to socialise with people who were in a similar position to mine. Once again, the money would be deducted from the DLA benefit I received, and paid directly to Headway.

Adam was my taxi for my first attendance. I was very apprehensive. Again, I wasn't particularly enthusiastic about going, but it was very easy to arrange, so I decided to give it a go.

I was wheeled in, and everybody was sitting around tables, talking to each other in their friendship groups. They turned their attention to the doors opening and saw me being wheeled through the door. Space was made at the end of the table, and I was told that they would go clockwise around the table, and each person would tell the group what they'd been up to.

There were about ten people before, and about ten people after me. Adam wheeled me into position and left.

Nobody else was in a wheelchair. They were all sitting, looking relaxed. Some were slouched in their seat, some were resting their elbows on the table resting their chin in their hands. One lad was sitting side-on to the table with his feet on a chair.

The cushion on my wheelchair meant that I was higher than everybody else. I was the only person sat bolt upright. I immediately stuck out. Nerves started to kick in, it felt like the first day of school. I was in a room full of people I didn't know.

I did a quick scan around the table and saw that nobody was physically disabled. I realised that my understanding of who would be attending this group, was completely misjudged.

Nobody would know I had speech problems. That I had trouble swallowing and needed to take intermittent breaths.

I began to panic about what to say; something I could say quickly so they weren't subjected to my boring voice. I rehearsed in my head as others were telling their stories. I had done nothing! I sat at home playing Football Manager or lying on the sofa watching TV.

This would have been the perfect opportunity to open up, with a captive audience and volunteers who were there to help people like me.

As always, I chose the easy route and said nothing beyond playing Football Manager and watching TV.

As some people around the table spoke there were heckles and participation from others. These people were obviously in a clique or popular amongst the group.

These were people who could speak properly. They had expression in their voices. They could change their tone. Their stories were entertaining. They could move freely, express themselves, their motions added to their story. I had no idea what their injury was, although just because you can't see a disability, doesn't mean there isn't an issue. Brain injuries can affect just about anything, and this was a brain injury charity after all.

Then people went and did what they wanted until the sandwich van delivered lunch. They'd generally play pool, board or card games or, fool around on the Nintendo Wii. Some went outside together to smoke.

They grouped together in their cliques, chatting and joking with friends.

Being the new boy, I hadn't formed any friendships. I needed to try, but in a wheelchair it's difficult to make connections when you can't circulate.

The chatter echoed around the room. People moved about, sometimes shouting to someone on the other side, sometimes turning to speak to someone as they walked by. I couldn't find a way to join in, being unable to speak loudly or quickly, and no one thought to approach or invite me.

Next at Headway was lunch. Each person put in two pounds and asked for the sandwich and crisps they fancied. Everybody strolled over and either sat with the group or grabbed their sandwich and stood around with their mates. I was wheeled over by a member of staff and space was made for me at the head of the table. I felt like the kid at school who nobody wants to talk to and just hangs around the teacher.

I attended for about three weeks and, with the Christmas break approaching, decided I wouldn't be returning. On the final day before the Christmas break there was talk of the Christmas party. Nobody mentioned it to me specifically, but I overheard people talking about it.

## All Clear

Since my operation in 2007, I'd had annual visits to see the Neurosurgeon, Professor Cruickshank. It was 2010 now, and my previous scans had shown a completely healthy brain.

Before I saw him, I had my annual MRI scan at the Birmingham Queen Elizabeth.

This time I wasn't serenaded with a pan pipe medley. Or if I was, I have no memory of it, with no choice but to listen to the 56k modem dialling up again.[33]

I knew I should have been apprehensive. It was possible it could trigger some PTSD and I'd have a panic

---

[33] My opinion that you're too young to know what a dial-up modem is still stands.

while I was in there. I had the same blasé attitude as before. I was sure nothing was going to be found then either.

I was almost nervous that I wasn't nervous.

I did feel fine now, and I wasn't experiencing any of the symptoms I was before. My previous idiocy was from having never experienced anything like this before.

The appointment was for 09:40am in Birmingham. My Dad took me, and the traffic was at a standstill for some of the journey. An ambulance zoomed up the hard shoulder, an accident had just occurred, it seemed. That brought back the memory of being taken to Stafford hospital from Cannock. Then came the memory of being transferred to the Haywood from the Q.E, and only being able to see out of the top of the window.

Even though we left my house at 08:00am, we still arrived a few minutes late. Luckily, I was seen fairly quickly.

Professor Cruickshank is like the Indiana Jones of neurosurgery in my opinion. Yet he sat behind his desk looking like a regular doctor. I doubt he wears a fedora and has a bullwhip, but I'm sure he has an alter ego.

He said that he was happy with the three scans I've had since the operation, there had been no change, so he was happy to discharge me. He said that I'm on file and if I have any questions or wish to see him, I can phone or make a priority appointment.

Asked if I had any questions, I asked was I likely to have another brain tumour? He said that I was no more likely than anyone else. It was unlikely, but not impossible.

Then I thought 'Maybe I should just check that I'm ok to fly.' I was flying to New Zealand in five days, I hadn't asked for any medical opinion as to whether it was safe to fly now.

My concern was the shunt that had been fitted to release pressure inside my cranium. As I would be subjecting it to a change in pressure, I had a sudden panic that my head would explode, or my eyes were going to pop out of my head.

Still unsure of exactly how the shunt worked, I garbled my question, grabbing fragmented breaths and holding my hand in front of my mouth to avoid spitting.

"In fivedays I'm goingtoNewZealand…I've gotobesatin a planeforhoursandhours I'm notgoingtobeabletostand I'm worried thatIshouldn't fly becauseoftheshunt. Isitsafe? I've alreadybookedthetickets."

Understandably Professor Cruickshank looked at me blankly and asked me to repeat myself. I wasn't ad-libbing now. I knew what I wanted to say. I slowly repeated the question and he confirmed there was nothing to worry about.

I was going to New Zealand, baby!

## New Zealand

This was a trip which had been planned for a while. Laura's brother Kev, and his partner Claire, had moved to New

Zealand a few years back and had quickly settled in and made a great life for themselves. We were to go out in January for three weeks.

Laura and her parents had flown out a year and a half previously following the birth of their first grandchild/nephew, but I didn't go as I didn't think I was going to be able to manage the long flight or staying in someone else's home. I was fairly sceptical about my ability to do it now, but I'd been trying to keep up appearances.

In hindsight everything changed on my first day home from hospital years ago. I was just delaying the inevitable. My girlfriend had become my part-time carer. I didn't do much, I barely ever left the house.

That couldn't be the case in New Zealand; I was going to have to be around people all the time; I couldn't hide away; I couldn't always rely on her for help. I was going to have to fend for myself as much as possible and when I did need help, I would have to be comfortable with asking for it.

Dad gave Laura and me a lift to the airport. Her parents made their own way down. Three weeks of luggage for four people, and five people in one car, wasn't going to work.

I'd told Dad we were flying from Heathrow. Fortunately, this came up in conversation before it became a problem.

"Isn't it Gatwick?" Laura asked.

"No, it's Heathrow," I confidently replied.

She picked up her mobile. "Hi Dad, are we flying from Heathrow or Gatwick? Yea I thought it was Gatwick… No, we'll be on time as we haven't got off the motorway yet."

Idiotic Tom strikes again!

When it came to boarding, I was wheeled up to the door of the plane, and I transferred into a narrower wheelchair that would fit into the aisle.

The staff were shown that the seat cushion and footplates of my chair could be removed. They folded and took it to be put into the hold.

I worried that I hadn't stressed how vital it was that the wheelchair didn't get lost, or that the cushion and footplates were just as important. I began to obsess, assuming my wheelchair wasn't a priority. I had no trust in the airport staff.

I didn't stress about it for very long. I saw that my seat had its own television screen that folded out of the left arm. Distracted like a toddler with shiny keys, I forgot my worries.

We sat at the front of the plane, where there was extra space and I could stretch my legs out, resting the soles of my feet against the partition between economy and business class.

The flight out would be twenty-eight hours with a stop at Incheon airport in South Korea where we would change planes. The return flight would be twenty-six hours plus a nineteen-hour sleepover in the airport hotel.

We arrived in Auckland to torrential rain, even though it was January, the height of summer in this part of the world. We'd dressed for hot weather.

Auckland was experiencing the tail end of horrific storms in Australia. Even though New Zealand is about 2,500 miles from Australia, the rainfall was biblical.

There were small lakes covering the car park. We could avoid some of them, but some had to be crossed. I was pushed straight through, able to hold my knees close to my chest to keep my feet dry, but the unfortunate pushing me got soaked.

We got to Kev and Claire's house. It was still tipping it down, but fortunately we were able to dive in through a basement entrance. We managed to shake off the majority of the water, and that's when I saw the stairs. Everybody went up and I shuffled up on my bum.

At the top I was helped into my chair and said hello for the first time to these strangers whose home I was a guest in.

You only get one chance to make a good first impression.

Bugger.

I'd never been this far afield before, and never had to deal with jet lag. I was advised to stave off sleep for as long as possible.

We were thirteen hours ahead of UK time. Sat bolt-upright in my seat, I hadn't slept a wink on the twenty-eight-hour flight. In business class, on the other side of the partition, they were lounging in their compartments, sipping drinks before pressing the button to turn their seat into a bed. I'm pretty sure I could have slept in those circumstances.

I made it to about 7:00 pm. Laura helped me transfer from the sofa into my wheelchair. As I was shattered I neglected to support my own weight, opting instead to lean heavily on her like a drunk trying to keep himself upright. She crumbled like a house of cards. I fell sideways, hitting my head on the wall. Fortunately, she dropped straight to the floor, and I didn't fall on her. She was unhurt.

I apologised and said "can I go to the loo?"

You only get one chance to make a good *second* impression.

Bugger.

The toilet was in a room on its own and with the previous failed transfer still fresh in the memory, I made sure I didn't make the same mistake again. I put my hands on her shoulders, stood up and turned to sit down on the toilet.

The toilet lid rested against the pipe connecting the bowl to the cistern. It was quite far to lean back, so I asked for something to prop against the pipe. A tray was found and I was left on my own. I leaned back and my makeshift backrest pushed the pipe out of its connection to the toilet.

Blissfully unaware, I pulled the chain and flooded the floor.

Bugger.

We went exploring most days and nights for the duration of our stay. It was a fantastic opportunity to see this amazing country, especially at this time of year. The sky was blue with barely a cloud. Most of the roads we encountered were single lane, sprawling through the untouched countryside. There weren't many cars. The only evidence that man is here is the stretch of asphalt you're currently travelling on. Everything seems to be green as far as the eye can see.

The people were incredibly friendly. The opportunity to holiday in New Zealand for three weeks without staying in a hotel with hundreds of other holidaymakers probably wasn't going to present itself again.

A highlight of the trip was our excursion to Mata Mata. Laura stayed behind, so her parents, Bob and Jean, came with me to see the place you'll probably know as Hobbiton from *The Lord of the Rings*. As we didn't pre-book, no disabled access had been prepared.

The weather was changeable and the lawns and flower beds weren't as neat and orderly as they were in the films. It was a struggle to get over the grass as the front wheels of the wheelchair kept hitting obstructions; the front wheels are basically trolley wheels, so even a small obstacle can be a problem.

The pathways, bordered by tape strung between poles, were often too narrow for the chair. I have to thank Bob and Jean for overcoming every obstacle, except for those that demanded extra hands. Typically for New Zealanders, there were always willing hands to help lift the wheelchair or even move the barriers.

Hobbiton is on the site of a working farm, requiring a fifteen-minute trip on a minibus as the site was huge. A tour guide stood at the front and told us about the history behind the set.

All of the sets were to be taken down when shooting was complete. But bad weather intervened every time an attempt was made to demolish Hobbiton. Eventually it was decided to leave it.

The bus parked by the entrance to the set and we were here.

The unkempt gardens and miserable weather didn't present the picture of Gandalf's cart meandering up the sunny lane to Bag End, but still, here I was in the Shire. To be here, on the other side of the world, seeing where Frodo jumped onto Gandalf's cart, where Bilbo said his birthday goodbye, should have been an impossible dream.

Peter Jackson avoided CGI anywhere that he could capture the real thing. Hobbiton is what you see on the films. Many of the Hobbit holes are set into the hills, with round doors and windows looking outwards. Everything is tiny, but the set itself is huge.

There is an old oak tree above Bag End. Again, Peter Jackson wanted to avoid using CGI, so a suitable oak was found near Mata Mata. All twenty-six tons of it had to be transferred to the set. He felt there weren't enough leaves on the tree, so thousands were hand-made and imported from Taiwan.

The enormous tree that provides the backdrop to Bilbo's party may look like CGI, but it's really there. It's a Monterey Pine, a type that doesn't grow in New Zealand. No one knows how it came to be here, but it's suspected that the seed was carried by a bird.

In spite of the difficulty to get me around the site, I managed to see everything I wanted to see. It's a day I'll never forget.

Our three week stay in New Zealand was fantastic. There were challenges as always, but it was a once-in-a-lifetime experience. I was in great company and Kev, Claire and their kids were brilliant hosts. The weather was generally stunning, but on the rare days where it was grey and gloomy it still had a fun holiday feel.

And you can't go wrong with a pool in the back garden and a mega-BBQ set up.

We left at six am for our flight back to the UK. I put on suntan lotion one last time, even though we were going to be in a car and then in an airport. We said our goodbyes and boarded the plane for the first leg of our journey, bound for Incheon Airport.

On arrival in South Korea, I was struck by the immaculateness of Incheon Airport. It looked like we were the first customers ever to use it.

Our room wasn't disabled-friendly, as I don't think we'd asked that it should be. I still hadn't got used to making special requests, preferring to try to maintain the illusion of normalcy. So it was my own fault that the bathroom door was to narrow for my wheelchair, that I needed to perch on the toilet to brush my teeth, struggling to balance on the highly polished lid. Or that Laura needed to unhook the shower head so that I could sit on the floor of the cubicle, washing my hair with one hand.

I shimmied out of the shower, dried myself and slid through to the bedroom and a welcome sleep.

The next day we flew on to the UK, where we were met by Dad for the drive home.

Laura's parents were away for a few more days, so she went over to their house to feed the cats. She returned as I was getting my lunch in the kitchen and told me it was over.

I'd thought something was different, both on the flight and the drive back home. We'd barely spoken. I'm sure this had been building for quite some time, and it must have been a heavy weight for her to keep it hidden.

In hindsight, the breakup was inevitable. Laura had stuck it out for two years, facing all sorts of changes to the life she'd signed up for. I don't blame her at all for leaving.

I tried to make it look like I wasn't too upset, but in truth I was. Not just because of the breakup, I was worried by what the future held for me.

Laura left to give me some time on my own. Mum came over and I told her the news. I fell to bits and had a bit of a cry. I think this was the first time in years that I'd shown any emotion.

I felt better for this immediately, it was good to get things off my chest.

The next couple of days were quite difficult' I realised I was stuck in the house unless somebody came round to get me. I found the nighttime quite difficult. Not just because I missed my girlfriend but because I felt so alone.

I phoned Dad and asked him to come and get me, and spent the night at their house.

# *Chapter 23 –Bring on Middle Age and Five Days in Sorrento*

So where am I now, I hear you ask. Well, I'm in my living room, sitting in front of my little fifteen-inch laptop that's on top of a portable table.

Actually, that's a bit flipping rude! WHAT BUSINESS OF YOURS IS IT WHERE I AM AT THE MOMENT? THAT IS FU… Oh, you meant where am I in life?

Thank you for asking. Please forgive my little outburst.

It's four days till my forty-first birthday. I started writing this book when I was thirty-eight, hoping to have it done by the time I was forty, so I could title this chapter, "life begins at forty." I missed that deadline, and there isn't a punchy phrase about being forty-one.

But it seemed more important to take my time rather than rush it, a trait I'd never had before. Now that I'm older and wiser[34], I realise there's time to do things, and not everything has to be done right away. I quite like this business of getting old. Life just seems easier. It's less stressful. It makes more sense seeing it through the eyes of a middle-aged man.

My real age has finally caught up to my already middle-aged dress sense. I don't have to try to dress in

---

[34] A bit less of an idiot might be more accurate.

attire that's suitable to my age. I can dress like a middle-aged man, without fear of ridicule. My hair is falling out; there isn't enough remaining to try and style it, Basically, get out of the shower, dry it and let it fall into the only style it can.

I'm naturally slower. I can't be bothered to rush into things, I give my brain a chance to tell me "That's an idiotic thing to do." I generally ignore it and do it anyway, but at least I'm now considering how idiotic I'm being. I'm comfortable with being in a wheelchair, I'm comfortable with how I sound. I'm comfortable with admitting I'm an idiot.

I feel like I know how this thing called life should be tackled now. I have a routine that is giving me the time to do things like trying to write this book.

Now that I'm middle-aged I get up earlier, but that makes me tired in the afternoon, I struggle to get through the day without a nap.

Oh, and I use a haemorrhoid ring every day. I haven't got piles, I stick my face in it. It helps in my recovery.

I should probably explain...

When I was attending Manchester Neurotherapy Centre, I was encouraged to spend time each day lying on my front, as sitting down all day can hurt your back and make your legs ache. Lying on your front gives your back and limbs a break.

I'm sure you're already thinking: 'Sounds like the perfect time to stick your face in a haemorrhoid ring.'

I Know! Great minds think alike. It really is a Godsend. My habit of jamming my left leg into the ground means this hour of recovery is vital. Plus, I can nap. Two birds, one stone.

The treatment table at Manchester had a cutout for the patient's face. My bedroom doesn't have the same equipment, but a haemorrhoid ring is a great substitute[35].

Writing this book has been great therapy. Therapy I think I've always needed but didn't pursue because I didn't want to have to talk. This was like a very long therapy session, so thanks for letting me bend your ear. Give yourself a pat on the back as you are probably the best therapist I've ever had. The bar was low though, you only had to keep your eyes open to get that accolade.

## Five Days in Sorrento

My brother Adam and his wife Ruth had booked a holiday in Positano followed by five days in Sorrento. It has been a long-held ambition of Dad's to see Pompeii, which isn't far away from there. They asked Dad if he wanted to join them in Sorrento, and I think Dad had booked the tickets before they finished asking the question.

We tend to come as a package deal nowadays, so I tagged along.

Thursday 22nd June 2023 arrived, and we started the drive down to Gatwick at midnight to get our 06:30am flight.

---

[35] Don't worry, it *is* a new one

There was no confusion as to whether Gatwick was the correct airport this time. All travel arrangements were kept from me because – and this is a direct quote – "You're a fucking idiot".

However, I guess the idiot gene runs in the family. This will become clear later.

We arrived at Gatwick at 03:00am. There was quite a small queue at security but as I'm in a wheelchair, I was able to skip it. I waved goodbye to all the losers in the queue, wiping the fake tears from my eyes as I was ushered precisely five metres further forward and told to wait to be searched.

I waved my blue badge in her face, but she didn't see this as proof I wasn't trying to smuggle something on board. I was frisked and my chair was dusted down.

My leather man-bag contained a deflated haemorrhoid ring, and this bothered them. I tried explaining that I stick my face through it when I lie on my front, but it didn't convince them I wasn't smuggling something. It had to go through the scanner.

We had hours to kill before our flight, so we went to get some breakfast. The menu at Wetherspoon's looked delicious. The queue didn't. We were told it was about an hour's wait for a table, but as I was getting special assistance we could sit in the special assistance lounge, order from the mobile app, and they would bring our food to us.

As it was four in the morning, we thought we'd be sensible and just order one beer each. Within about ten minutes our breakfast arrived, along with our beer.

Holiday mode: engaged.

They'd provided us with an electronic device to tell us when we should report for boarding. At the bleep, we went to the assistance desk and waited with a few other people.

You've probably seen those electric cars that carry disabled people to the boarding gates. They look like the Johnny Cabs from Total Recall. We were looking forward to sailing past the pedestrians, waving regally and treating them to our smug expressions.

The reality was ever so slightly different. There wasn't room for everyone, but the driver generously invited us to walk[36] behind.

The Johnny Cabs don't look that fast, but hurtling through the airport, clutching my man-bag with the haemorrhoid ring, while my 71-year-old father galloped like a demented rickshaw driver suggests otherwise.

While waiting, we'd struck up conversation with a lady who, seated comfortably in one of the rear-facing seats, watched the performance with obvious enjoyment. Boarding was incredibly quick and easy. I don't fly much but as I understand it's never this simple. I presume this was because of the special assistance. The whole experience was stress-free, we got to have a nice breakfast, sit away from the crowds and were left with plenty of time to board.

---

[36] run

A short flight later and we were at Naples International Airport. The heat was incredible! The thin layer of hair left on my head, was instantly drenched in sweat. I didn't realise it was this hot in Italy.

The airport staff had suddenly changed into catalogue models with designer stubble.

There seemed to be some sort of industrial strike going on. Everybody was lined up on the tarmac, in the baking sun, queuing to file inside and go through one of just two open check-in desks. The carved-from-marble, designer-stubbled catalogue model guided us past the queues, barking "Mi scusi" and sliced through to passport control in minutes. A marooned flight crew tagged along behind us, saying "We usually walk past all this."

I'm sure you've noticed that I haven't spoken about the toilet yet[37]. Don't worry, we're back to my usual topic...

We followed a sign for disabled toilets. What we found didn't have any grab rails, or indeed any apparatus that would satisfy the description.

There wasn't a toilet seat either.

I rolled straight out and tried the disabled toilet next door. It was also lacking in any accessibility fittings. Or a toilet seat.

After about twenty minutes on the Autostrada, we spent the remainder of the journey to Sorrento on single lane

---

[37] For the real enthusiast, there's a lot about my Italian toilet experience at www.sorrentno.com.

roads, twisting along the coast with sheer rock faces on the left.

The traffic moved at about twenty miles an hour, allowing us to catch glimpses of amazing views to our right between the bushes and tree branches. The intensely blue Mediterranean stretched to the horizon. Mount Vesuvius was some distance away but clear as day. Its peak was shrouded in cloud against a cloudless sky. Far below, dozens of boats, yachts and super-yachts, rocked in the blue. People clustered around roadside fruit stands or just gazed out to sea.

As the cars crawled forward, mopeds and scooters darted in and out at frightening speed. They'd overtake on blind bends, straddling the white line until they met another moped coming the other way. They'd then somehow find space among the cars to avoid death. Everyone wore helmets, but were dressed in tee shirts and shorts. Had there been an accident, the injuries would have been horrific.

But there never was an accident, at least while we were there. And in this heat, wearing leathers wouldn't be an attractive option.

We arrived at our apartment, parked the car in the courtyard, and arranged to have pre-dinner drinks with Adam and Ruth.

At the agreed time, we headed off to meet them at a bar in the main square. Almost every street in Sorrento is cobbled, not ideal for wheelchairs, but they look gorgeous. Exactly how I pictured Italy – like when Michael Corleone flees to Sicily in *The Godfather.*

Walking down the narrow alleys and side streets offered a view into the rear of shops. People would be chatting in Italian, mopeds outside the open door. We found wider stretches with restaurants on one side and an outside seating area of another restaurant on the opposite side. Music played almost everywhere.

We found Adam and Ruth at the bar in Piazza Tiasso. Adam surprised us by ordering drinks in Italian, and then chatting amiably and apparently fluently with the waiter. We had no idea he spoke Italian, but in fairness he'd been there nearly a week. He's like that.

I sat with a big grin on my face, 'this is exactly how I pictured Italy' I thought. I sipped on Aperol Spritz and munched on snacks.

As early evening came on, the heat of the day changed to gentle warmth. We walked through golden light across the square to the restaurant.

Seated outside, on the edge of Piazza Tiasso, among tables that were nicely spaced for privacy, we surveyed the menu.

The food in Italy is incredible. It's my favourite cuisine, but the Italian restaurants I've been in at home don't do it justice.

Every ingredient is so fresh it tastes like the vegetables have just come out of the ground. All pasta has just been made by hand, specifically for your meal. Every pizza made in Italy was crafted just for you.

An important lesson I learnt is that cheese isn't a default ingredient of pizza in Italy. If it doesn't say cheese on the menu, your pizza won't have it.

We finished the night as we finished almost every night – sitting on the terrace of Adam and Ruth's hotel, overlooking the Mediterranean Sea. Far below us, boats were moored for the night on their jetties. In the bay, yachts, some of them ablaze with lights on every mast, rocked gently at anchor. Headlights appeared and disappeared in the distance as cars navigated the mountain roads.

The operation that changed so much in my life was sixteen years in the past. I still need a wheelchair, and my speech isn't likely to get me a job as a newsreader, but seeing old videos makes me realise how far I've come. I'm far more independent than I was just a couple of years ago. Life has changed, but so does everyone else's – they're just different changes.

I look out at Vesuvius, a dark shape against the sky. Music plays softly and, cocktail in hand, I think back to Doctor Soryal's words all those years ago.

"There definitely will be quality of life in the future".

He was right.

\*\*\*

Fast forward to five days later; we're standing in the car park back at Gatwick Airport at 02:00am, searching our bags for the car key. It's nowhere to be found. Dad says he checked the keys were in the bag before we left.

I say – and this is a direct quote – "He's a fucking idiot".

Printed in Great Britain
by Amazon